Back to Basics
HARVEST

By Suzanne Massee

This book is copyright. Apart from any fair dealing for the purpose of private study, research, criticism or review, as permitted under the Copyright Act, no part may be reproduced by any process without prior permission of Suzanne Massee.

© Suzanne Massee 2010

Designed by: Tigerzi Design

ISBN 978-0-6483675-1-2 Paperback

ISBN 978-0-6483420-8-3 Hardcover

2nd edition 2018

Dedicated to the Universe

May we enjoy the fruits, the memories of the season's harvest, of what Mother Nature provides around the universe each season for all to savour.

Acknowledgements

I express my sincere thanks to all those who shared their collection of recipes, and to those whose recipes have been sitting in archives, waiting to be dusted and rejuvenated.

Thank you for making possible collection for others to enjoy.

Contents

Introduction 7
Chutney or Relish 8
Preparation of Chutney 8
Safe Food Practices 9
Chutney and Relishes 11
Sauce 29
Mustards 33
Preparation of Jams 39
Conserve 43
Marmalade 47
Jam's 51
Jellies 59
Syrups 67
Fruit Butters and Pastes 71
Curd's 74
Specialties and Pickled 77
Liqueurs and Brandied fruit 82
Vinaigrettes and Pesto 85
Herbal Oils and Vinegars 88
Preserving Fruit and Vegetables 90
Fresh Chutneys and Sauces 96
Mayonnaise and Sauce 101
Dairy Products 104
Conversion Chart 110
Index 111

Introduction to the Harvest

What could be more natural than to go out into the garden and pick nature's own flavours?

There is nothing more satisfying than adding these ingredients to the pot: the natural vitamins and minerals that fill the air with their aromas.

I have accumulated years of recipes and knowledge that I want to see passed on to our children and children's children before all this knowledge is lost.

Daily we watch the global advance of commercial packet foods and fast food outlets and engineered foods as they encroach into our daily life, our health system and finally into our planet Earth.

With home preserving you can create your food just the way you like it: you are in control.

Preserving is not difficult, and what could be more satisfying than knowing that what you are consuming is preservative-, additive-, colour-, rancid fat-, over-salt-, emulsifier-, genetic engineering- and spray-free. Wow! I know my choice.

Fruit can be picked locally and you have the choice of what you harvest.

I always remember visiting my grand mum, and the wonderful aromas and tastes in her kitchen; adoring the wonderful dill pickles straight from the barrel. My only downfall was not understanding Polish and as a child not being able to say "No!" - so there was a many an overdose of pickles!

I have always had a naturally ability to savour the flavours in recipes and know if ingredients are missing in the mix, before it has even been put into the pot: wonderful gift when you are in the food industry.

Let your imagination harvest wonderful delights.

Food is an enjoyable basis for interaction when shared with friends; it's good to share knowledge about what is grown and produced in our country.

I have created this "Back to Basics Harvest" book in steps for ease of use and to show you when to add ingredients throughout the cooking process.

Chutney or Relish

I am often asked about the difference between chutney and relish.

Relishes originated from India and resemble chutney, but they are more highly-spiced and can be made into a sweet and sour puree made from sweet and sour vegetables with the addition of pickled onions and gherkins.

Chutneys date back to the British colonial era and are similar to the relish, but have more recognisable pieces of fruit and vegetables.

Piccalilli is an English pickle consisting of small florets of vegetables preserved in a spicy mustard and vinegar sauce.

Recently added to the preserve list is onion jam or onion marmalade. This is a trendy new twist to the humble chutney.

Chutneys, relishes and piccalilli are all enjoyed and add value to cold meats, vegetables, cheese spreads, and sandwiches ... the list is endless.

Chutneys are a wonderful casserole-enhancer. Just add up to half a jar of chutney to a casserole with your favourite meat and vegetables and bake, or add to a stew when cooking.

Preparation of Chutney

Size of preserving pan should be 10 litres or more, for ease of use.

Chutneys are best cooked in large quantities, as reduction is slower, the acids from the vinegar are greatly reduced, and the flavours of all the fruits and spices used are enhanced.

Sterilise clean jars in the oven for 15 minutes or more at 100C.

Lids that have intact seal grip on used jars are excellent for re-using. Replace lids that show any sign of damage.

Sterilise the lids by bringing a saucepan of water to the boil and immersing the lids for 10 - 15 minutes.

Always wipe spills around the rim of the jar with a clean cloth.

If you do not have lids, you can seal with jam preserve cellophane: wet one side and place wet side down over the jar, and fasten with a rubber band. As the cellophane dries it will shrink and form a seal.

Fruit and onions can be processed in a food processor, using the chipper blade, or prepared by hand. Cut vegetables into bite-sized pieces.

Always remember to stir the bottom of the pan frequently to prevent the chutney sticking to the pan bottom and burning.

Sultanas are normally added near the end of cooking as they particularly tend to stick and burn.

Chutneys are reduced to a thick consistency, although not too thick to pour into the jars.

To bottle chutney have one jug to scoop out ingredients and pour into a second jug that is used for filling the jars. I have always found beer jugs have a good pouring spout; use a fork to guide the pulp into the jars.

Clean the rims of the jars to allow the seal grip to seal to the jar.

Label and date.

Chutneys are like a wine: they need to age. Normally after six months chutneys lose that vinegar taste; kept for a year or more, the characteristics of the chutney will mellow into warm subtle flavours.

Safe Food Practices

Main causes of food deterioration

- Poor food hygiene • Lack of temperature control
- Unclean jars • Jars not sterilised
- Fruit is not thoroughly washed.
- Using over-ripe or decayed fruit. • Seal on jar has not adhered.

Chutney and Relishes

Apricot Chutney

- 3 kg apricots • 1.5 kg onions
- 450 g raisins • 900 g sugar
- 40 g white mustard seeds
- ½ teaspoon chilli powder
- 1 litre white vinegar
- 1 teaspoon ground cinnamon
- 1 tablespoon turmeric • 350 ml lemon juice • 1 cup slivered almonds

De-stone apricots, peel and chop onions. Place all ingredients into pan except almonds.

Bring to boil and simmer for 1 hour or until thick.

Remember to stir the bottom of the pan frequently!

Add almonds, then bottle in sterilised jars.

Cherry Chutney

- 4.5 kg cherries pitted • 700 g currants
- 400 g brown sugar • 250 g golden syrup
- 1.2 litres white vinegar • 2 tablespoons ground allspice

Hand-chop cherries for a chunky style or place in food processor with vinegar and finely chop.

Place all ingredients into pan; bring to the boil stirring until the sugar dissolves.

Simmer for 1½ hours. This chutney can be slightly runny - the flavours are superb.

Remember to stir the bottom of the pan frequently!

Pour into sterilised jars.

Feijoa Chutney

- 3 kg feijoas • 1.5 kg onions
- 1.5 kg apples • 700 ml white vinegar
- 3 teaspoons mixed spice
- 3 teaspoons ground ginger
- 3 teaspoons ground cloves
- 3 teaspoons ground nutmeg
- 1.2 kg sugar • 1 teaspoon cayenne pepper • 3 tablespoons salt

Chop feijoas with skin on, peel and chop onions, core and chop apples with the skin on.

Place all ingredients into a large pot. Bring to the boil and simmer for 1 ½ to 2 hours until thick.

Remember to stir the bottom of the pan frequently!

Pour into sterilised jars.

Pear Chutney

- 4 kg pears • 1 kg apples • 400 g onions • 120 g fresh ginger
- 20 g garlic cloves • 1 tablespoon chilli powder
- 1 ½ teaspoons ground cardamom • ¾ teaspoon cayenne pepper
- ½ teaspoon ground cinnamon • 1 kg brown sugar
- 1.4 litres white vinegar • 700 ml water • 160 ml lemon juice
- 850 g sultanas

Peel, core and chop pears, core and chop apples, peel and chop onions, finely-chop ginger and garlic. Place all ingredients except sultanas into pan. Bring to boil and simmer for 2 hours, add sultanas and cook for a further 30 minutes to an hour until thickened.

Remember to stir the bottom of the pan frequently; more frequently with this chutney as it will stick to the bottom of the pan and burn.

Pour into sterilised jars.

Plum Chutney

- 2 kg red plums
- 2.5 litres white vinegar
- 2 x 410 g tins peeled tomatoes
- 600 g onions • 600 g carrots
- 400 g apples • 750 g brown sugar
- 2 tablespoons rock salt
- 250 g raisins

In a muslin bag add

- 2 cinnamon quills
- ½ tablespoon whole cloves
- 5 dried chillies • 2 star anise
- 1 tablespoon whole black peppercorns

Tie bag and place in pan.

De-stone plums. Peel and grate carrots. Peel, core and chop apples. Peel and chop onions. Add all ingredients to pan except raisins, and simmer for 2 hours. Add raisins and cook for up to 1 hour.

Remember to stir the bottom of the pan frequently!

Take out muslin bag and discard.

Pour into sterilised jars.

Prune and Apple Chutney

- 3 kg apples • 500 g prunes • 200 ml lemon juice • 600 g sugar
- 2 teaspoons ground nutmeg • 700 ml white vinegar

Peel core and chop apples. Add all ingredients to the pan and bring to the boil, stirring until the sugar dissolves. Simmer until thick: about 30 minutes to 1 hour.

Remember to stir the bottom of the pan frequently!

Pour into sterilised jars.

Tamarillo Chutney

- 3 kg tamarillos
- 1 kg apples
- 1 kg onions
- 2 kg sugar
- 2 tablespoons salt
- 6 tablespoons mixed spice
- 1 teaspoon cayenne pepper
- 1 litre white vinegar
- 1 cup chopped crystallised ginger
- 2 x 425 g tins crushed pineapple
- 500 g sultanas

Peel and chop tamarillos. Core apples and chop with the skin on. Peel and chop onions.

Place all ingredients except the sultanas into a large pot and bring to the boil. Simmer for 1 hour, add the sultanas and simmer for 1 more hour.

Bottle when mixture thickens.

Remember to stir the bottom of the pan frequently!

Pour into sterilised jars.

Hint: To peel tamarillos easily, bring water to the boil in a large pot, take off heat and place the tamarillos into the hot water. The tamarillo skin will split, allowing it to be easily peeled with a knife.

Ajvar

(Serbian relish, pronounced as eye'var)

- 3 kg red capsicums, de-seeded
- 250 g fresh red chillies, de-seeded
- 4.5 kg eggplant, peeled
- 1.5 litres white vinegar
- 4.5 litres water
- ½ cup salt

Bring to the boil vinegar, water and salt. Blanch the eggplants, peppers and chillies for 5 minutes.

Drain blanched vegetables.

Place blanched vegetables into a food processor with • 5 tablespoons of rock salt • 1 teaspoon paprika • 2 cups of cooking oil, and process all vegetables and mix altogether.

In a large pan add • 150 g chopped garlic and • 260 ml of cooking oil and fry. Do not brown the garlic. Add the processed vegetables, bring to the boil and simmer for 15 minutes, stirring often.

Pour into sterilised jars.

How to use Ajvar:

Ajvar makes a wonderful dip for raw or blanched vegetables or topping for fish, chicken, turkey or baked potatoes.

Ajvar produces a wonderful soft apricot colour.

Mix it with plain yogurt to make a salad dressing.

Add chopped roasted almonds for a chunky sauce.

Mix through yoghurt cream cheese (page 107) and use as a dip.

Tamarind Relish

- 1.5 kg tamarind

Soak in 3 litres of hot water for 1 to 3 hours; when cool strain the pulp through a sieve or a large-holed sieve similar to a chip basket. Set aside.

In a large pan add

- ½ tablespoon crushed dried chillies
- 4 tablespoons crushed whole cumin
- 3 tablespoons turmeric
- 2 tablespoons mustard seeds
- 1 cup cooking oil
- 1.5 kg onions peeled and chopped
- 3 tablespoons garlic peeled and chopped
- 1 cup chopped fresh ginger

Fry altogether until soft, add the sieved tamarind pulp and

- 1.25 litres white vinegar
- 6 cups of sugar
- 1 kg of dates
- ½ cup salt

Bring to the boil and simmer for 1 hour or until thick.

Mixture can be bottled with pulp texture or use a stick blender to make a puree.

Remember to stir the bottom of the pan frequently!

Pour into clean sterilised jars.

Maharajah's Relish

- 3 kg bottled or tinned peaches • 1.25 kg peeled chopped onions
- 1.25 litres white vinegar • 900 g sugar • 750 g dates
- 150 g chopped crystallised ginger • 250 g mixed peel
- ¼ cup salt • 2 heaped tablespoons curry powder
- 1½ teaspoons cayenne pepper • 1 tablespoon dried crushed chillies

Place all the above ingredients into a large pan and bring to the boil. Simmer for 2 to 3 hours.

Blend together with a stick blender - or use a potato masher to make a smoother pulp mixture.

Remember to stir the bottom of the pan frequently!

Pour into clean sterilised jars.

Maharajah relish makes an excellent sauce: puree ingredients with a blender and bottle.

Hot Indian Relish

- 1.4 kg apples, peeled and chopped
- 900 g onions, peeled and chopped
- 1.4 kg brown sugar
- 2.8 litres white vinegar • 900 g raisins
- 8 cloves garlic peeled and chopped
- 4 tablespoons salt • ½ teaspoons cayenne pepper
- 4 tablespoons ground ginger • 6 tablespoons mustard seeds
- 4 tablespoons paprika • 2 tablespoons ground coriander seeds

Place all the ingredients in a large pan, bring to the boil, simmer up to 2 hours or until the mixture is thick.

Remember to stir the bottom of the pan frequently.

Pour into clean sterilized jars.

Brinjal Pickle

(Indian aubergine pickle) Very Hot

- 5 kg aubergines chopped into small chip size (or use the chip blade with a food processor).

Place aubergines into an old pillow-case. Sprinkle 2 heaped dessert-spoons of salt and turmeric over aubergines. Place pillow-case on a colander to drain, and leave for 30 minutes to draw the juice out of the aubergines. Press pillow-case to drain as much liquid as possible.

- 180 g mustard seeds
- 180 g dried chillies
- 60 g turmeric
- 60 g cumin seeds
- 500 g fresh ginger
- 300 g peeled garlic
- 1 litre white vinegar

Place all the above ingredients into a food processor and process into a pulp.

- 3 litres mustard oil (available from selected Indian food outlets)
- 1 litre white vinegar

Into a large pot add a litre of the mustard oil, heat the oil and fry all the pulped spice until aromatic, adding more mustard oil to prevent a dry mixture. Add to this the drained eggplant and the rest of the mustard oil and the vinegar.

Bring to the boil and simmer approximately 30 minutes or until the oil floats on top.

Remember to stir the bottom of the pan frequently!

Pour into clean sterilized jars.

Zucchini Chutney

This chutney is wonderful when the zucchini season is out of control.

- 800 g tomatoes skinned and chopped or 2 x 410 g tins whole peeled tomatoes

- 2.8 kg zucchini chopped into small chunks

- 450 g onions peeled and chopped • 2 tablespoons salt

- 2 tablespoons ground ginger • 2 tablespoons ground black pepper

- 1 tablespoon ground allspice • 800 g sugar • 1.5 litres white vinegar

Place all ingredients into a large pot. Bring to the boil and simmer up to 2 hours or until mixture is thick.

Remember to stir the bottom of the pan frequently!

Pour into clean sterilized jars.

Ratatouille Chutney

- 2 kg tomatoes skinned and chopped or 5 x 410g tins whole peeled tomatoes

- 1 kg onions peeled and chopped • 1 kg eggplant chopped

- 1 kg zucchini chopped • 4 green peppers de-seeded and chopped

- 6 garlic cloves peeled and chopped

- 150 g fresh chopped chillies and seeds or 2 tablespoons chilli powder

- 2 tablespoons salt • 1 tablespoon ground cloves

Place the ingredients in a large pan; bring gently to a simmer with the lid on until vegetables are soft. Add to this

- 1 kg sugar • 1 litre white vinegar

Bring to the boil and simmer with lid off until chutney is thick.

Remember to stir the bottom of the pan frequently!

Pour into clean sterilized jars.

Rhubarb Chutney

Goes well with cold and hot meats, with cheese board and as a sandwich spread.

- 2 kg rhubarb chopped • 4 onions peeled and chopped
- 4 oranges: the juice, grated skin and flesh, but not the pith
- 5 garlic cloves peeled and chopped • 200 g raisins
- 1 litre white vinegar • 1 kg sugar • 1 teaspoon mustard seeds
- 1 teaspoon ground coriander • 1 teaspoon ground ginger
- 1 teaspoon ground allspice • 2 teaspoons salt

Place all ingredients into a large pot, bring to the boil and reduce to a simmer until thick and pulpy - about 1 ½ hours.

Remember to stir the bottom of the pan frequently!

Pour into clean sterilized jars.

Banana and Date Chutney

Banana date chutney is excellent with curries.

- 2 kg bananas • 2 kg apples, cored and chopped
- 1 kg dates, chopped • 4 oranges, blended in a food processor
- 1.5 tablespoons mixed spice • 1.5 tablespoons ground ginger
- 1.5 tablespoons curry powder • 1.5 tablespoons salt
- 1.8 litres white vinegar • 1 kg sugar

Place all ingredients into a large pot and bring to the boil. Reduce heat and simmer for 1 hour.

Remember to stir the bottom of the pan frequently.

Lightly blend with a stick blender or mash with a potato masher.

Pour into clean sterilised jars.

Onion Marmalade

- 7.5 kg onions peeled and sliced • 6 bay leaves
- 100 g black mustard seeds • 70 mls cooking oil • 8 mls mustard oil

Place all the ingredients in a large pan, fry and sweat on a low heat with the lid on for up to one hour.

Add to this 750 g sliced oranges and sweat for half an hour with lid on pot.

Now add: • 2.25 g brown sugar • 1.5 litres water

- 1.5 litres white wine (cask wine is the most cost-effective)

Bring to the boil and reduce to a simmer.

When the mixture has reduced to half the liquid it is ready to bottle.

You may wish to use a potato masher lightly to get the ingredients to blend slightly, or leave as is. This is a slightly runny texture.

Onion marmalade goes well on any dish or even added to casseroles and stews.

Aubergine and Capsicum Relish

- 2 kg red capsicums • 2 kg apples • 4 kg onions
- 150 g fresh chillies and seeds • 300 g fresh ginger
- 5 tablespoons ground coriander seeds • 2.5 litres vinegar

De-seed capsicums and chop. Core apples and chop. Peel onions and chop. Finely-chop ginger and chillies. Place all ingredients into a large pot, bring to the boil and simmer with lid on until onions are soft.

Add to this mixture

- 650 g sultanas • 1.8 kg sugar • 4 teaspoons salt
- 3 kg aubergines unpeeled and chopped into small chip size

Simmer until mixture becomes thick.

Remember to stir the bottom of the pan frequently!

Pour into sterilised jars.

Chilli Jam

- 2 kg red capsicums, de-seeded
- 120 g whole fresh chillies, de-seeded

Place the capsicums and chillies into a food processor and blend until fine.

In a large pot blend 70 g of pectin with the processed capsicum and chillies with 1 litre of water.

Bring to a simmer, and slowly add:

- 4 kg sugar • 700 g dextrose

Bring to the boil and simmer for 30 minutes, then add:

- 1 litre white vinegar • 15 ml citric acid • 1 ¼ tablespoons salt

Bring back to a rolling simmer for 1 hour to 1.5 hours until the consistency is like jam.

Let the pot sit for 30 minutes to cool slightly.

Pour into clean sterilised jars.

Chilli jam is a sweet heat flavour and is wonderful with cheese boards, on toast, over ice-cream, in yoghurt, over cream cheese, on fish and egg omelettes, added to sorbets, served with chocolate fondues or on mouse traps ... the list is endless.

This next recipe was the public's favourite in a Wine/Food Challenge regional competition in 2003. Contestants were required to match wine and food; this dish was an outstanding dessert wine match.

Suzanne's Lime chilli cheesecake

Serves 10 – 12

Base • 2 packets gingernut biscuits, crushed

• 250 g butter melted • 1 teaspoon cinnamon

Mix together all the base ingredients, place into a 28cm ring tin.

Filling • 500g cream cheese • 1 tin condensed milk

• 2 fresh red chillies de-seeded and finely chopped

• 1 ¼ cups lime juice (lemon juice may be substituted for lime juice, although it will not be quite as good)

• 2 teaspoons gelatine dissolved in 100 ml of hot water

• 500 ml whipped cream

Beat the cream cheese until fluffy, add condensed milk and beat to combine. Add the chillies, lime juice and gelatine, and mix to combine. Fold in the whipped cream.

Pour onto the base and leave to set. Top with chilli jam.

Lime and Date Chutney

Lime and date chutney is excellent with curries. This chutney is best left for up to six months or more; the flavour is then outstanding.

• 2 kg whole limes, sliced • 2 kg apples, cored and chopped

• 1 kg dates, chopped • 1.5 tablespoons mixed spice

• 1.5 tablespoons ground ginger • 1.5 tablespoons curry powder

• 1.5 tablespoons salt • 1.8 litres white vinegar • 1 kg sugar

Place all ingredients into a large pot and soak overnight.

Bring to the boil, reduce heat and simmer for 1 to 2 hours until tender and mixture is thick. Remember to stir the bottom of the pan frequently!

Pour into clean sterilised jars.

Quince Chutney

- 9 large quince, peeled and chopped • 1 ½ cups raisins
- 2 x 410 g tins whole peeled tomatoes • 1.5 kg sugar • 1.5 kg apples, peeled and chopped • 6 onions, peeled and chopped
- 9 dried chillies crushed • 3 tablespoons salt
- 1 ½ tablespoons ground ginger • ¾ teaspoon cayenne pepper
- 1 ½ teaspoons mustard powder • 1 ½ teaspoons curry powder
- 2.25 litres white vinegar

Place all ingredients into a large pan, bring to the boil, reduce heat and simmer for 1 to 2 hours until tender and mixture is thick.

Remember to stir the bottom of the pan frequently!

Pour into clean sterilised jars.

Quince chutney can be made into a quince sauce by blending to a puree with a food processor or hand held blender.

Carrot and Mustard Seed Chutney

The orange colour is retained in this very edible chutney.

Serve on savoury scones or with cheese and cold meats.

- 3 kg carrots, peeled and finely grated • 1. 5 litres water
- 10 tablespoons mustard seeds • 5 tablespoons salt
- 1 ¼ teaspoon cayenne pepper • 1 cup lemon juice
- 200 g grated fresh ginger • 1.5 litres white vinegar

Put all the ingredients into a pot, and leave to soak overnight.

Bring to a boil and simmer for 20 minutes.

Then add: 2 kg sugar

Simmer for 30 minutes or until mixture is thick. (This is a slightly runny texture).

Remember to stir the bottom of the pan frequently!

Pour into clean sterilised jars.

Beetroot and Orange Chutney

3 kg beetroot

Clean and wash beetroot, place in a large pot filled with water, bring to the boil, and then reduce to a simmer. Take off heat and drain when beetroot skin comes away from the beetroot easily. You can use your hands to squish the skin off.

Chop beetroot into bite-sized pieces or put through using the food processor chipper blade. Place in clean large pot with 2 grated orange skins, flesh and juice, but not the pith.

(You may wish to peel the skin with a potato peeler and chop it up.)

In a muslin bag with a stone to weigh it down, place

- 2 cinnamon sticks
- 3 teaspoons whole allspice
- 5 cm bruised whole ginger
- 2 teaspoons black peppercorns
- 6 bay leaves

Tie bag and place in with the beetroot and orange juice and peel.

- Pour in 1.5 litres white vinegar • 4 tablespoons salt • 2 kg sugar

Bring to the boil and simmer for 60 minutes until mixture's liquid has reduced slightly. Take off heat and remove muslin bag.

You may wish to use a potato masher lightly to blend the ingredients slightly, or leave as is.

Remember to stir the bottom of the pan frequently!

Pour into clean sterilised jars.

Kiwi Fruit Chutney

- 2 kg kiwi fruit, peeled and chopped
- 100 g crystallised ginger, chopped
- 6 onions, peeled and chopped
- 1 cup raisins • Juice of 2 lemons
- 1 teaspoon ground ginger
- ¼ teaspoon cayenne pepper • 1 cup sugar • 2 cups white vinegar
- 1 dessert spoon salt • 6 garlic cloves, skinned and chopped

Place all ingredients into a large pot and simmer gently for up to 2 hours, or until thick and pulpy.

Remember to stir the bottom of the pan frequently!

Pour into clean sterilised jars.

Soda Bread

A bread that is quick to make in no time using no yeast. Enjoy it for a weekend brunch with chutney and poached egg ... or serve hot with jam.

- 450 g white flour • 1 teaspoon baking soda • 1 teaspoon salt
- 1 teaspoon cream of tartar • 300 ml milk

- ½ cup chopped fresh herbs (optional)

Sieve dry ingredients, make a well and add milk slowly to the mix.

Dough should be pliable to knead. Knead until smooth.

Make into a loaf, or a cob shape, or make into round buns.

Score a cross on the top with a knife.

Or make savoury pin wheels: pat out flat and spread with chutney. Gather one end and roll to form a log, slice portions up to 4cm thick and lay them flat side up. Sprinkle with grated cheese.

Bake loaf at 190c for 40 minutes – pin wheels for up to 20 minutes.

Green Tomato Chutney

This chutney is wonderful way to use all those un-ripe tomatoes.

- 1.5kg green tomatoes sliced thinly
- 450g pears or apples peeled, cored and chopped
- 250g onions peeled and chopped
- 225g sultanas
- 225g dates
- 225g brown sugar
- 2 teaspoons salt
- 450ml white vinegar
- 1 tablespoon ginger finely chopped
- 1/2 teaspoon cayenne pepper
- 1 teaspoon mixed spice
- 1 teaspoon mustard powder

Place all ingredients into pan; bring to the boil and simmer for about 2 hours or until thick.

Remember to stir the bottom of the pan frequently!

Pour into sterilised jars.

Sauce

Rhubarb Chilli Sauce

- 2 kg rhubarb • 60 g garlic • 500 g onion • 300 g red peppers
- 650 g sugar • 2 teaspoons salt • 3 ½ teaspoons cayenne pepper
- 2 tablespoons tomato paste • 1 tin, approx 400g, crushed pineapple
- 2 teaspoons grated fresh ginger • 2 ½ litres white vinegar
- 250 g fresh chillies and seeds

Clean and chop rhubarb, onions, red peppers and garlic. Put all ingredients into a large pan, bring to the boil and simmer for 30 minutes to 1 hour. Use a stick blender or process in a food processor until smooth or a thick pulp.

Pour into hot sterilised jars. This sauce has a "sweet-heat" flavour.

Garlic Sauce

(similar to Worcestershire sauce)

- 6 litres white vinegar • 500 g treacle
- 120 g salt • 300 g garlic, chopped
- 150 g fresh ginger, chopped
- 1.5 kg onions, peeled and chopped • 750 g brown sugar

Place the ingredients into a large pot.

In a muslin bag add,

- 15 g dried chillies • 30 g whole cloves

Place a clean rock in the bag to weigh down, tie the bag and place in pot. Stand pot over night to release flavours.

Bring to the boil and simmer for an hour. Take out muslin bag and discard. Whiz ingredients with a stick blender or process in batches in a food processor.

Pour into clean sterilised jars.

Blackboy Peach or Plum Sauce

- 4 kg plums or peaches, de-stoned • 2 litres vinegar or to cover fruit
- 1.2 kg sugar • 1 ½ teaspoons cayenne pepper • 2 ½ tablespoons salt
- ½ teaspoon ground cloves • 1 tablespoon ground ginger
- 1 ½ teaspoon ground black pepper • 1 ½ teaspoon mace*
- 80 g garlic, peeled • 1 ½ tablespoons hot curry powder
- ½ cup dried oregano or 1 cup fresh oregano

Place all ingredients into a large pot, bring to the boil, reduce heat and simmer for 2 to 3 hours.

Whiz ingredients with a stick blender or process in batches in a food processor to make a sauce puree.

Remember to stir the bottom of the pan frequently!

Pour into clean sterilised jars.

Hint: To de-stone plums, cook plums in the vinegar until soft, then leave to cool. Use your hands to squeeze the stones away from the plum flesh, or place in batches into a large sieve and sieve the stones out.

*Mace is the outer coating of a nutmeg seed; to replace mace use nutmeg.

Tomato Sauce

- 6 kg tomatoes, skinned and chopped • 25 g ground allspice
- 500 g onions, peeled and chopped • 100 g salt • 25 g ground cloves
- 1 teaspoon mustard powder • ¼ teaspoon cayenne pepper
- 1 kg sugar • 8 garlic cloves, peeled and chopped
- 450 ml white vinegar

Place all ingredients into a large pot, bring to the boil, and simmer for an hour. Process with a kitchen stick blender, or in batches in food processor, or through a sieve.

Return to the heat and simmer for up to 30 minutes or until mixture thickens. Pour into clean sterilised jars.

Red Tomato Sauce

This sauce retains the rich red colour, and is very similar to the commercial variety - but far better for you.

The ingredients in the second part of the recipe are available from the chemist; some chemists have them already made up for the tomato sauce recipe. If not, the required amount is below.

- 6 kg tomatoes • 5 large onions, peeled and chopped
- 50 g garlic cloves, peeled and chopped
- 2 teaspoons ground ginger • ½ teaspoon cayenne pepper
- 4 tablespoons salt • 2 teaspoons ground black pepper
- 1.25 kg sugar

Place the above ingredients into a large pot and bring to the boil. Simmer for 2 hours.

Put the sauce through a sieve, forcing through as much as possible of the pulp.

Return to the heat and boil for 30 minutes

Add these ingredients to the sauce and mix:

- 45 ml glacial acetic acid • 3 ½mls oil of cloves
- 15mls spirits of wine or refined or rectified spirit

(or the store-bought mixture). Pour into clean sterilised jars.

Mustard seeds when crushed with water, juice or vinegar release a volatile and piquant essence which gives the mustard a distinct flavour.

There are three varieties of mustard seeds: black mustard, which is spicy and piquant; brown mustard, which is less piquant; and white mustard, which is not very piquant but more bitter and pungent.

Dijon mustard is named from the main centre of production in Dijon in France.

Mustards are very simple to make and take little time; all you need is a food processer to break the mustard seeds.

Mustards go well with cold and hot meats, in sandwiches, added to sauces for macaroni cheese or in fact any sauce dish. Try mustard coated on the steak before or after grilling, or added to homemade vinaigrette.

Mustards

Vinaigrette

Here's a quick and simple vinaigrette: mix a teaspoon of mustard with a tablespoon of vinegar and top with 100 ml of either rice bran, olive or vegetable oil. Salt and pepper to taste. Drizzle over hot vegetables or on salads.

Pine nut and Almond Mustard

- 400 g white mustard seeds
- 200 g black mustard seeds
- 450 litres white vinegar
- 700 ml grape juice
- 1 tablespoon rock salt
- ¾ teaspoon ground cumin
- 100 g pine nuts
- 150 g slivered almonds

Place all ingredients except pine nuts and almonds into a plastic bucket and soak for 48 hours. Place soaked seeds into a food processor and process for 2 minutes to coarsely grind the mustard seeds. Add the nuts and process further until coarsely broken. Don't over process: do just enough to break the nuts.

Pour into clean sterilized jars.

Red Wine Mustard

- 300 g white mustard seeds • 300 g black mustard seeds
- 1 litre red wine • 50 ml fresh chopped parsley • 25 ml celery seeds
- 50 ml dried tarragon • 4 whole garlic cloves • 10 anchovy fillets
- 2 teaspoons rock salt

Place all ingredients into a plastic bucket, soak for 48 hours.

Place all ingredients into a food processor and process for 2 minutes. Rest for 2 hours. Re-process for a further 4 to 5 minutes.

Pour into clean sterilized jars.

Herb and Spice Mustard

- 300 g black mustard seeds • 300 g white mustard seeds
- 1 litre grape juice • ¼ teaspoon ground cloves
- 1 teaspoon ground black peppercorns • 2 teaspoons ground ginger
- 100 ml dried or fresh tarragon • 2 teaspoons ground nutmeg
- 1 teaspoon dried or fresh thyme • 1 ½ tablespoons ground cinnamon
- 20 g garlic cloves chopped • 10 bay leaves • 1 ½ teaspoons rock salt

Soak all ingredients in a plastic container for 48 hours. Process in food processor for 3 minutes. Rest for 3 hours, then process for a further 5 minutes.

Pour into clean sterilized jars.

Guinness Mustard

- 250 g black mustard seeds • 700 g white mustard seeds
- 1 bottle Guinness • 600 ml red wine vinegar
- 1 teaspoon ground cinnamon • 1 teaspoon ground cloves
- 1 teaspoon ground nutmeg • 1 teaspoon ground allspice
- 3 ½ tablespoons rock salt
- 1 ½ tablespoons ground black peppercorns

Soak all ingredients in a plastic bucket for 48 hours. Process in food processor until coarsely ground.

Pour into clean sterilized jars.

Anchovy Mustard

- 600 g black mustard seeds • 600 g white mustard seeds
- 1 litre grape juice • 1 teaspoon ground cloves
- 1 teaspoon ground black peppercorns • 2 teaspoons ground ginger
- 200 ml fresh or dried tarragon • 2 teaspoons ground nutmeg
- 1 teaspoon fresh or dried thyme • 1 ½ tablespoons ground cinnamon
- 20 g garlic cloves, chopped • 10 bay leaves
- 25 g rock salt • 1 jar anchovies (approx 80 g)
- 7 egg whites and yolks

Soak all ingredients except the anchovies and eggs in a plastic bucket for 48 hours. Process in food processor for 4 minutes, add the anchovies and eggs, process for a further 4 minutes.

Pour into clean sterilized jars.

Green Peppercorn Mustard

- 600 g black mustard seeds
- 600 g white mustard seeds
- 1 litre grape juice
- ½ teaspoon ground cloves
- 1 teaspoon ground black peppercorns
- 2 teaspoons ground ginger
- 200 ml fresh or dried tarragon
- 1 ½ teaspoon ground nutmeg
- 1 teaspoon dried or fresh thyme
- 1 ¼ tablespoons ground cinnamon
- 20 g garlic cloves chopped
- 10 bay leaves
- 25 g rock salt
- 200 g green peppercorns

Soak all ingredients except the green peppercorns in a plastic bucket for 48 hours. Process in food processor for 4 minutes, add green peppercorns and process for up to 2 minutes until the peppercorns are slightly broken.

Pour into clean sterilized jars.

Mustard fruits

Mustard fruits are a wonderful "sweet-heat" accompaniment to antipasto dishes, or served with cold meats or delicious just straight out of the jar.

Dried fruit listed below is a guide; make up your fruit mixture to your own taste. Mustard oil is available at selected Indian food outlets.

Syrup

- 1 litre water • 1 kg sugar • 2 large whole chillies split

Bring to the boil and simmer for 30 minutes.

Place dried fruit mustard seeds and mustard oil into each sterilized jar

- 2 whole prunes
- 2 mangoes
- 4 apricots
- 2 cranberries
- 4 crystallised ginger
- 1 pear
- 2 pineapple
- 2 papaya
- 1 fig
- 1 teaspoon mustard seeds
- 2 tablespoons mustard oil

Into each jar pour in the syrup, seal each jar and leave to infuse for 6 weeks. I have found mustard fruits keep well for more than 2 years.

Preparation of Jams

Jam is produced by taking mashed or chopped fruit and boiling it with sugar and water.

Conserve is a jam made up of whole fruits, which are retained in their whole form.

It's myth that overripe fruit can be used for jam. The best jam set is achieved by using slightly under-ripe fruit as it has more pectin and higher acid levels.

Hints for jam making

Sugar proportions vary with the type of fruit and its ripeness. In most jams, equal weights of fruit and sugar are used.

Bring fruit to a boil and simmer slowly until the fruit is tender. Add the sugar, and bring back to a rapid boil. When the temperature reaches 104C or 219F the acid and the pectin in the fruit react with the sugar. The jam will set on cooling.

Testing

To test for jam set, chill a couple of saucers in the freezer. Drop small jam samples on the saucers, and place back into the freezer. Test after 30 seconds or when the samples are slightly cool. A skin should form and wrinkle on the top when you touch it with your finger; or run your finger through the sample: if the jam runs together it needs further boiling. If it doesn't, the jam is ready to bottle.

Jar sterilisation and preparation

Use the same principles as for chutney preparation on page 8

Pectin

Pectin produces the stiffness in jams that makes them set.

Under-ripe fruit has more pectin than fully-ripe fruit. To make jams without adding commercial pectin, the fruit ratio to use is 25% under-ripe fruit and 75% ripe fruit.

Fruits that are high in pectin are apples, citrus, gooseberries, currants and quince.

Low pectin fruits are raspberries and strawberries.

Pectin can be extracted from high pectin fruits and added to low pectin fruits to help set jams and reduce cooking time.

Pectin is extracted from the pith in citrus skins, apple skin and cores or, in the case of quince, the whole fruit.

The skin and core of apples can be added to the pot in a muslin bag while cooking to extract the pectin in low-pectin fruit jams.

Marmalade jams are soaked overnight to extract the pectin, and the cooking extracts more pectin.

Commercial pectins are an easy form of pectin to use for jam set. Jams using commercial pectin require less cooking time.

Adding a small knob of butter to the ingredients will help reduce the foaming that is created when using commercial pectin or high pectin fruits.

Home-made pectin

Pectin can be extracted from high pectin fruits: apples, quince, gooseberries and red currants.

Place whole fruit chopped 1 kg to a pot of 750ml of water, bring to the boil and simmer for up to 1 hour until pulped. Strain through a jelly bag.

To test pectin strength, place in a cup 1 teaspoon of liquid with 3 teaspoons of methylated spirits. Swirl the contents and allow to cool, and drain off the methylated spirits. If the remainder forms a clot the pectin is high: if it separates the liquid needs further cooking.

Pectin ratio to use is 300 ml to 2 kg of low pectin fruit.

Acid in jams

Acid is needed in jam-making for flavour and gel set.

Acid is higher in under-ripe fruits. Most fruits have enough acid content - although some recipes do call for lemon juice or citric acid to be added.

Sugar

Sugar is a preservative and helps with the setting of the jam.

Problems with fruit and jam

Fruit is floating: due to fruit not having been cooked enough before adding the sugar, or the jam not being rested long enough before bottling.

Fruit is tough: fruit has not been cooked long enough before the sugar was added.

Jam is runny: setting of the jam has not been achieved. Reheat it slowly bring back to the boil and re-test for jam set.

Conserve

Boysenberry and Cointreau Conserve

- 3 kg boysenberries • 3 kg sugar

- 3 cups lemon juice • 1 cup cointreau

Place boysenberries and lemon juice into a large pan, bring to a boil and reduce to a simmer until the boysenberries are soft. Add the sugar and bring to a rapid boil for about half an hour.

Test for jam set. Leave to cool 10 to 20 minutes and add the Cointreau.

Remember to stir the bottom of the pan frequently!

Pour into clean sterilised jars.

Cherry and Kirsch Conserve

- 3 kg cherries pitted
- 500ml lemon juice
- 1.75 kg sugar
- 150 ml kirsch

Place cherries and lemon juice into a large pan and cook until fruit is soft. Add the sugar and bring to a rapid boil for about half an hour. Test for jam set. Leave to cool 10 to 20 minutes and add the kirsch.

Remember to stir the bottom of the pan frequently!

Pour into clean sterilised jars.

Blueberry and Grand Marnier Conserve

- 2 kg blueberries
- 100 ml lemon juice
- 25 ml white vinegar

Place blueberries, lemon juice and vinegar into a large pot, bring to the boil and simmer until fruit is soft.

Add • 900 g sugar

Bring back to the boil and simmer until a jam set is achieved.

Cool slightly and add • 100ml Grand Marnier.

Remember to stir the bottom of the pan frequently.

Pour into clean sterilised jars.

Enjoy the conserves together with yoghurt cream cheese (page 107) on fresh bread or toast.

The conserves add decadence to a home-made sponge with whipped cream

Home-made Sponge with conserve

- 175 g sugar

- 2 tablespoons water

Place sugar and water in a saucepan and bring to the boil without stirring until sugar has dissolved.

- 4 eggs, separated.

- ½ teaspoon vanilla essence or 1 teaspoon finely grated lemon rind.

Beat egg whites to form peaks, add the syrup of sugar and water while still warm, and beat to mix.

Add egg yolks, vanilla essence or lemon zest and beat for 15 minutes.

Sift together

- 175 g cornflour

- 1 dessertspoon plain flour.

Sprinkle this over the beaten eggs and fold it into them, using a large spoon. (You may use the beater on slow beat, but avoid over-beating to avoid knocking too much air out of the mixture.)

Pour into a ring tin, well-greased and flour-dusted inside. You may wish to line the base with grease proof paper.

Bake 190C for about 20 minutes or until the sponge starts to come away from the sides.

Allow to cool slightly and place onto cake rack.

Serve with lashings of whipped cream and conserve or your favourite jam.

Marmalade

Grapefruit and Ginger Marmalade

- 1 kg sliced grapefruit • 1 kg sliced lemon • 1 kg grated carrot
- 6 litres water • 250 g fresh ginger chopped

Soak the grapefruit, lemons, carrots, ginger and water overnight.

Bring mixture to the boil and boil for up to 3 hours.

Weigh the pulp.

Add • 1.35 kg of sugar to every 1 kg of pulp.

Add the sugar and bring back to the boil, boil until clear and a jam set has been achieved.

Cool slightly. Remember to stir the bottom of the pan frequently.

Pour into clean sterilised jars.

Orange and Almond Marmalade

- 1.5 kg oranges or (use Seville oranges, a bitter orange used in marmalades) • 1 kg lemons • 5 litres water

Slice oranges and lemons, place in pot with water and soak overnight.

Bring to the boil and simmer until fruit is soft.

- Add 4 kg of sugar.

Bring to the boil and boil until you have a jam set, cool slightly.

- Add 1 cup sliced almonds.

Remember to stir the bottom of the pan frequently.

Pour into clean sterilised jars.

Lime Marmalade

- 2 kg limes sliced • 3 litres water

Place limes and water in a large pan and soak overnight.

Bring to the boil with the lid on and simmer until rind is soft.

Add to this :

- 3.5 kg approx sugar (1 cup of sugar to 1 cup of pulp)

Bring back to a boil and simmer without the lid on, until you have a jam set. Remember to stir the bottom of the pan frequently.

Pour into clean sterilised jars.

Coconut bread and lime marmalade are the ideal partners for a weekend breakfast treat. (page 49)

Coconut Bread

This cake is mentioned with the lime marmalade.

- 2 eggs • 300 ml milk • 1 tsp vanilla • 2 ½ cups flour
- 2 tsp baking powder • 2 tsp cinnamon • 1 cup caster sugar
- 150 g coconut • 75 g melted butter

Lightly whisk egg, milk and vanilla, and add to dry ingredients. Add melted butter and stir until mixture is smooth. Do not over-mix!

Bake 180C 1 hour. Cool in tins 5 mins.

Orange Marmalade Cake

- 6 eggs • 200 g sugar • 300 g ground almonds
- 1 tsp baking powder • 100ml Grand Marnier
- 1 orange 2 lemons boiled whole for 45 mins and pureed

Beat the eggs until light and creamy; add sugar, almonds and baking powder.

Continue beating until soft peaks form. Add the pureed citrus. When well-mixed add the liqueur and pour into lined tin. Bake at 180C for 1 hour.

Remove from oven and cool for 20 mins before turning out.

Glaze: In saucepan melt • 200g orange and almond marmalade (page 47) with • 100ml of Grand Marnier. Simmer, stirring until ingredients combine and sauce becomes syrupy (about 3 minutes).

Pour over cake, and garnish with toasted slivered almonds.

Serve with whipped cream, home-made crème fraiche or mascarpone (on page 104 and 105, or store-bought).

This cake is excellent hot or cold

Melon and Ginger Jam

Pie melon is a heritage heirloom plant which, in years gone by, was used as a filling in pies and to extend jam volumes. If you happen to come across this melon, which looks similar to the honey dew melon, have a go and make this recipe;

It is quite delicious.

- 3 kg melons peeled, de-seeded and chopped using the food processor chipper blade

- 750 ml lemon juice • 1 litre water

Soak melons, lemon juice and water overnight.

Bring pot to the boil and simmer with the lid on until the melons become transparent (about 1 hour).

To this add:

- 3 kg sugar • 750 g crystallised ginger, lightly chopped.

Bring back to the boil and simmer without the lid on, until you get a jam set (about 1 hour).

Remember to stir the bottom of the pan frequently!

Pour into clean sterilised jars.

Pear Ginger Jam

- 2 kg pears peeled, cored and chopped using the food processor chipper blade.
- 400 g chopped crystallised ginger
- 100 ml lemon juice
- 2 kg sugar

Place all ingredients into a large pot and soak overnight.

Bring to the boil and simmer for up to 2 hours or until a jam set is achieved.

Take care with this jam as it is liable to stick and burn to the bottom of the pot:

Stir the bottom of the pot frequently!

Pour into clean sterilised jars.

Summer Berry Jam

- 1 kg strawberries
- 1 kg raspberries
- 1 kg boysenberries
- 200mls lemon juice

Place berries and lemon juice into a pot, and heat over a low heat until fruit is soft.

Add • 3 kg sugar and bring to a rapid boil, testing at 10-minute intervals for a jam set.

Remember to stir the bottom of the pan frequently!

Pour into clean sterilised jars.

Apricot Jam

- 3 kg apricots, de-stoned
- 150ml lemon juice

Place apricots and lemon juice into a large pot and cook slowly until fruit is soft and pulpy.

Add to this

- 3 kg sugar

Bring to a boil and simmer until a jam set.

Take care with this jam as it is liable to stick and burn to the bottom of the pot: Stir the bottom of the pot frequently!

Pour into clean sterilised jars.

Black Doris Jam

- 3 kg black Doris plums, de-stoned and cut into quarters
- 150ml lemon juice

Place plums and lemon juice into a large pot and cook slowly until fruit is soft and pulpy.

Add to this

- 3 kg sugar

Bring to the boil and simmer until a jam set is achieved.

Remember to stir the bottom of the pan frequently!

Pour into clean sterilised jars.

Feijoa and Ginger Jam

- 3.6 kg feijoas, sliced with skin on • 800 ml water
- Juice and rind of 6 lemons

Place the ingredients into a large pot and bring to the boil; simmer until the feijoa skins are soft.

Add: • 2.4 kg sugar • 250 g crystallised ginger, chopped

Bring to the boil stirring until sugar has dissolved.

Bring back to the boil and simmer until a jam set is achieved.

Remember to stir the bottom of the pan frequently.

Pour into clean sterilised jars.

Blackcurrant Jam

- 3.5 kg blackcurrants • 3 litres water

Place blackcurrants and water in a large pot, bring to a boil and simmer until fruit is soft.

Add to this

- 4.65 kg sugar

Bring back to the boil and simmer until you get a jam set.

Remember to stir the bottom of the pan frequently.

Pour into clean sterilised jars.

Strawberry and Rhubarb Jam

- 1 kg rhubarb, chopped • 2 kg strawberries • 1 cup lemon juice
- 3 kg sugar

Place rhubarb, strawberries and lemon juice into a plastic container, and sprinkle over with the sugar. Leave overnight to juice up.

Bring to the boil, stirring until boiling point to avoid fruit sticking to the pot bottom, then boil for up to 30 minutes or until jam sets.

Pour into clean sterilised jars.

Strawberry Jam

- 3 kg strawberries, hulled
- 1 cup lemon juice
- 2.5 kg sugar

Place strawberries, lemon juice and sugar into a large pot, and leave to stand overnight.

Add • two grated apples peeled and cored (this is for added pectin).

Bring to the boil and simmer slowly for approximately 45 minutes or until you have a jam set.

Remember to stir the bottom of the pan frequently.

Pour into clean sterilised jars.

Jam Tarts

Pastry

- 250g flour
- 60g caster sugar
- Pinch salt
- 180g butter
- 2 egg yolks
- Few drops water

In a food processor, combine the flour, sugar and salt, add butter, and process until it resembles breadcrumbs. Add egg yolks and water. Knead and cover. Refrigerate 1 hour. Roll out pastry, place in a pie dish, prick the base with a fork all over to prevent shrinkage, and bake for about 15 minutes or until lightly golden at 200C.

Pour your favourite jam onto the baked pastry, place in oven for 10 minutes until jam is hot.

Serve with whipped cream and ice-cream.

Scones with Home-made Jam

- 3 cups plain flour • 6 teaspoons baking powder • pinch salt
- 150 g butter, grated • 300ml milk

Sieve the flour, salt and baking powder into a large bowl, add the butter and rub slightly into the flour so the mixture looks like grated cheese throughout.

Add the milk and fold through lightly.

Put onto a floured board and knead lightly to mix. Butter will retain a grated appearance.

Pat mixture out on an oven tray, making rectangle cuts to form rough scone shapes.

Bake 200C for about 15 minutes.

Or make scone cut-out shapes, or form a log and slice into 2cm thickness. Or pat flat into a round shape and score the top into wedges.

Serve with jam and cream.

Savoury Scones with Chutney

This scone mix is excellent for savoury scones. Roll out flat spread with chutney and add grated tasty cheese, ¼ teaspoon paprika and chopped fresh herbs onto scone mix. Gather one end and roll to form a log, slice into 2 cm thicknesses, and place flat on baking tray to resemble pin wheels and bake. Serve with butter and your favourite chutney.

Variation: add salami and bacon to the cheese mixture; the chutney is optional.

Berry Jam with Stevia

Stevia rebaudiana: a natural sweetener alternative. Stevia grows well and when dried grinds to a fine powder in a coffee grinder. It is available from health food outlets. Stevia in a powder is 300 times sweeter than sugar!

Berry Jam

- 500 g raspberries • 500 g strawberries • 500 g boysenberries

Place in a pot with juice of • 1 lemon and • 1 cup of water. Bring to the boil, reduce heat and simmer until fruit has separated. Add up to • 1 teaspoon or more of stevia, then take a small amount and do a taste test. Add • 50ml of glycerine, stir into jam, and bottle. Seal the jars, as this jam does not have the keeping qualities of jam made with sugar. Refrigerate.

This is a syrupy jam and has a full intense flavour of berry fruits.

To make a thicker jam, add • 4 tablespoons of agar or gelatine when the fruit has separated. Stir in well and proceed with the stevia and glycerine.

Apple and Chocolate Jam

Apple and chocolate jam is enjoyed on toast, over ice-cream, with pancakes and waffles.

- 3.5 kg apples • 2 kg sugar • 200 ml lemon juice
- 2 cups water • 1 tablespoon vanilla essence

Peel and core apples, placing the cores and peel into a muslin bag for more pectin.

Place all ingredients into a large pot. Bring to a boil then reduce to a simmer until apples are soft and pulpy.

Blend with a hand blender stick or in a food processor. Return mixture back to pot and heat.

Add:

- 150 g cocoa blended with hot water to mix. • 250 g dark chocolate

Simmer this mixture until it resembles a thick sauce.

Remember to stir the bottom of the pan frequently.

Pour into clean sterilised jars.

Jellies

Jellies are translucent, and use the juice of the fruit. When spooned onto a plate a good jelly holds its shape. Jellies have a wide range of flavours, from sweet to savoury.

Jelly bags are available from specialty shops, although I prefer to use an old pillowcase.

Scald the bag in boiling water before using.

Place the open damp bag in a pot and pour the pulp in carefully. Now tie the bag to the broom stick and lift it onto the chair bridge.

Place two upright chairs back to back, about a metre apart. Rest a broomstick on the backs like a bridge, and hang the bag to drip freely into a large pot overnight.

Do not squeeze the bag as this will make the jelly cloudy.

Leave to drip overnight.

Pectin content

Measure the juice back into a large pot, take a sample and test for pectin, as follows:

Put 1 teaspoon of the cooled juice into a bowl, add 3 teaspoons methylated spirits, stir the mixture and leave for a minute. If a large jelly clot forms the fruit is high in pectin; if a smaller clot forms it is lower.

Sugar is added on pectin content.

High pectin add 2 cups sugar for every 2 ½ cups juice

Low pectin add 1 ½ cups sugar for every 2 ½ cups juice

Bring to the boil and stir to dissolve the sugar.

Boil rapidly without stirring until setting point is reached.

Herb Jellies: Rosemary, Mint, Thyme, and Marjoram Jelly

Fill large pot ¾ full with chopped whole apples; add water to barely cover apples.

For mint, rosemary, thyme or marjoram jelly place a very large bunch of that particular fresh herb into the pot.

3 large lemons, chopped

Bring to the boil and simmer with the lid on until apple is soft and pulpy. Stir in 1 cup of white vinegar.

Pour carefully into a jelly bag and leave to drip overnight.

Check pectin content.

Measure juice back into pot and add the appropriate amount of sugar.

Bring to the boil and stir to dissolve the sugar.

Boil rapidly without stirring until setting point is reached.

Continue to boil rapidly without stirring until jam set.

To each clean sterilised jar add fresh herb leaves chopped or whole, to decorate and add more flavour to the jelly.

Pour into clean sterilised jars.

Rose Geranium Jelly and Lemon Verbena Jelly

Fill large pot ¾ full with chopped whole apples; add water to barely cover apples.

Place a very large bunch of fresh geranium or lemon verbena into the pot.

3 large lemons, chopped.

Bring to the boil and simmer with the lid on until apple is soft and pulpy

Pour carefully into a jelly bag and leave to drip overnight.

Check pectin content.

Measure juice back into pot and add appropriate amount of sugar.

Bring to the boil and stir to dissolve the sugar. Boil rapidly without stirring until setting point is reached. Boil rapidly without stirring until jam set.

To each clean sterilised jar add a fresh geranium leaf or lemon verbena to decorate and add more flavour to the jelly.

Pour into clean sterilised jars.

(NB: Geranium pelargonium scented varieties produce volatile oils and aromas for the food and perfumery industries.)

Feijoa Jelly

Fill large pot ¾ full with whole chopped feijoas; add water to barely cover fruit.

- Add 3 lemons, chopped • 4 large apples, chopped

Bring to the boil and simmer with the lid on until feijoas are soft and pulpy. Pour carefully into a jelly bag and leave to drip overnight.

Check pectin content.

Measure juice back into pot and add appropriate amount of sugar. Bring to the boil and stir to dissolve the sugar. Boil rapidly without stirring until setting point is reached.

Pour into clean sterilised jars.

Hawthorn Jelly

This is a bitter-sweet flavour which goes well with lamb and game as well as scones and cream.

Place • 2 kg chopped whole apples into a pot; add • 1.5 kg hawthorn berries and water to barely cover apples and • 1 large lemon, chopped.

Bring to the boil and simmer with the lid on until apple is soft and pulpy.

Pour carefully into a jelly bag and leave to drip overnight.

Check pectin content.

Measure juice back into pot and add the appropriate amount of sugar.

Bring to the boil and stir to dissolve the sugar, then boil rapidly without stirring until setting point is reached.

Pour jelly into clean sterilised jars and seal.

Rose Petal Jelly

Use to fill sponge cakes, or enjoy with scones and cream.

Place • 2 kg chopped whole apples into a pot with • 1 x 10 cm cinnamon stick, • 1 large chopped lemon, • 2 cups rose hips and water to barely cover ingredients.

Bring to the boil and simmer with the lid on until apple is soft and pulpy.

Pour carefully into a jelly bag and leave to drip overnight.

Check pectin content.

Measure juice back into pot and add appropriate amount of sugar.

Bring to the boil and stir to dissolve the sugar, add • 25 g rose petals.

Boil rapidly; stirring until setting point is reached.

Pour jelly into clean sterilised jars and seal.

Crab Apple Jelly

Fill large pot ¾ full with whole crab apples; add water to barely cover apples. Add 3 lemons, chopped.

Bring to the boil and simmer with the lid on until apple is soft and pulpy.

Pour carefully into a jelly bag and leave to drip overnight.

Check pectin content.

Measure juice back into pot and add appropriate amount of sugar.

Bring to the boil and stir to dissolve the sugar.

Boil rapidly without stirring until setting point is reached.

Pour into clean sterilised jars.

Quince Jelly

Fill large pot ¾ full with whole chopped quince; add water to barely cover fruit.

- Add 3 lemons, chopped

Bring to the boil and simmer with the lid on until quince is soft and pulpy.

Pour carefully into a jelly bag and leave to drip overnight.

Check pectin content.

Measure juice back into pot and add appropriate amount of sugar. Bring to the boil and stir to dissolve the sugar.

Boil rapidly without stirring until setting point is reached.

Pour into clean sterilised jars.

Grape Jelly

This was one of my favourites among the jams my grand mother made. Grand mum used to keep boiling the jam until it got to this over-cooked or burnt jam stage. It was more of a syrup jam, but it was so Ohh! Divine! Make as for jellies but continue cooking until it looks similar to golden syrup. It does take quite a bit of cooking, but have some fun ... it is yummy!

Place grapes into a large pan, crush down and add 6 large chopped apples and 3 chopped lemons and enough water to barely cover fruit.

Bring to the boil and simmer until fruit is pulpy.

Strain through a jelly bag overnight. Check pectin content.

Measure juice back into pot and add appropriate amount of sugar.

Bring to the boil and stir to dissolve the sugar.

Boil rapidly without stirring until setting point is reached.

Pour into clean sterilised jars.

Loquat Jelly

Place loquats in a large pot and fill with water to barley cover the fruit; add 1 chopped lemon. Bring to the boil and simmer for up to 1½ hours until fruit is pulpy.

Take off heat; pour into a jelly bag, and leave to drain.

Check pectin content.

Measure juice back into pot and add appropriate amount of sugar. Bring to the boil and stir to dissolve the sugar.

Boil rapidly without stirring until setting point is reached.

Pour into clean sterilised jars.

Steamed Sponge Pudding with Jelly

- ½ cup home made jelly or jam of choice • 175 g self-raising flour
- 75 g butter • 50 g caster sugar • Zest of 1 lemon
- Pinch salt • 1 egg • 100 ml milk

Grease a 1 litre pudding basin. Pour the jelly of choice into the bottom of the basin.

In a mixing bowl add the butter, caster sugar, lemon zest and salt. Rub the ingredients together until they resemble breadcrumbs.

Mix the egg and milk together, pour this into the flour and beat altogether for 10 minutes until smooth.

Pour mixture over jelly or jam.

Place greaseproof paper or tinfoil over basin and secure with a string or with the pudding basin lid.

In a large pot, place a trivet or an upturned saucer to keep the pudding basin off the bottom.

Pour in boiling water to cover two thirds of the sides of the pudding basin. Cover pot with a lid and simmer over a low heat for 1½ hours.

Check the water level periodically and add as necessary to keep a constant level.

Take off heat, remove foil or greaseproof paper.

Place a plate on top and turn the pudding upside down.

Serve with ice-cream or whipped cream.

Steamed Sponge Pudding with Jelly Oven Method

Make as for recipe above, but omit placing batter mixture into a pudding basin.

Grease 6 small ramekins, and place a spoonful of jam or jelly in the bottom of each one. Pour mixture onto jam to ¾-fill each ramekin, then cover it with tinfoil and secure with an elastic band.

Place moulds in baking dish half-filled with boiling water.

Bake at 200C for 30 minutes.

Syrups

Syrups make excellent ice-cream toppings. Dilute them with hot or cold water to taste for a refreshing drink.

Rose Hip Syrup

This syrup is rich in Vitamin C. Use undiluted with yoghurts or as a sauce over ice-cream and puddings. Dilute in hot water as a refreshing tea. As a tonic drink, take one dessertspoon a day.

- 2.5 kg rosehips • 5.5 litres water

Bring water to the boil. Mince the rose hips in a blender, place into boiling water, and boil for 30 minutes. Draw pan aside and rest for 1 hour. Pour into a jelly bag and leave to drain.

Measure the total amount of juice back into a clean pot.

For every 750 ml of juice add 500 g of sugar or to taste.

Bring to the boil and boil for 5 minutes.

Pour into clean sterilised jars. This syrup can be used immediately and will keep for up to 1 year.

Lemon Syrup

- 675 g sugar   • 1 litre lemon juice. • Grated rind of 3 lemons

Place all ingredients into a large pot and bring to a simmer. Strain the syrup through a muslin cloth, and bottle into clean sterilised bottles.

Orange Syrup

Make as for lemon syrup, replacing lemon juice with orange juice and add juice of 2 lemons.

Grape Juice

Place grapes into a large pot and cover with water, bring to the boil. Take off heat and use a potato masher to pulp the grapes.

Place into a jelly bag and leave to drain.

Bring juice to the boil; this may be bottled at this stage.

Or add sugar for sweetening:

250 g sugar to every litre of juice. Bring back to a simmer until sugar has dissolved.

Pour into clean sterilised jars.

Black Currant Syrup

- 2 kg sugar • 1¼ litres water

Bring to the boil and boil 10 minutes.

Add • 1½ kg of black currants, bring to the boil and boil for a further 10 minutes, then strain and bottle into clean sterilised jars.

Strawberry Sauce

This sauce is excellent over ice-cream, or use as a filling in desserts.

- 1 kg strawberries • 900g sugar • 175 mls red wine vinegar

Place all ingredients into a bowl. Lightly mash strawberries, and leave to macerate overnight.

Place into a large pot, bring to the boil, and boil for 15 minutes until it thickens.

Pour into clean sterilised jars.

Blackberry Syrup

Excellent winter cough and cold remedy.

- 2 kg blackberries • 1 cinnamon stick • 150 ml water

Place blackberries with water and cinnamon stick into a large pot, set at a low heat and simmer until fruit is pulpy and soft. Strain through a sieve, place back onto the heat and add.

- 600 g honey or sugar

Bring back to a boil and boil for 10 minutes.

Pour syrup into clean sterilised jars and seal.

Fruit Butters and Pastes

Butters are a lovely spread to enjoy with bread, toast, scones and cream.

Pastes are an enjoyable sweetmeat served in slices with cheese, or maybe stirred into gravy before serving to add that little bit of difference.

Fruit butters and pastes are fruit pulps cooked with sugar until all liquid has evaporated.

Fruit pastes are a further reduction: the butters are cooked until the mixture is dry.

Butters and pastes do not require a setting test.

Pulp that is left over from jelly-making goes well for butters and pastes.

Butters and pastes can be poured into a grease lined container to cool and dry. When dry cut into wedge portions, and place into lined containers with a lid. This way, they will keep up to a year.

For each 225 g of fruit pulp add 175 g sugar.

To test, place a spoonful onto a plate: there should be no liquid coming away from the pulp. It is then ready to pour into containers.

Stir over a low heat until sugar has dissolved. Pastes and butters require quite a bit of stirring as they will stick to the bottom of the pan, and be aware: it can spit.

Plum Butter

- 2 kg plums de-seeded • 2 cups water

Bring to the boil and simmer with lid on until plums are pulpy. Place through a sieve or use a stick blender or food processor.

Weigh pulp. Place into pot with sugar measurement.

Bring slowly to the boil and stir until sugar has dissolved. Simmer, stirring frequently until thick, with no excess liquid.

Pour into clean sterilised containers.

Plum Paste

Make as for plum butter but continue cooking until the paste thickens and begins to come away from the bottom of the pan, stirring continually. Be aware: boiling paste will spit.

Take off heat and continue stirring until spitting stops. Pour paste into shallow baking dish and leave to cool.

Leave covered with cloth and place in a cylinder cupboard for a few days until dried.

Slice into portions and Glad wrap. Store in air-tight container.

Apple and Blackberry Butter

- 2 kg apples peeled and cored • 1 cup water • 1 kg blackberries

Simmer apples, black berries and water until soft, then pass through a sieve. Weigh fruit and for every kilo add 750 g sugar.

Bring slowly to the boil and stir until sugar has dissolved. Simmer, stirring frequently until thick, with no excess liquid (about 20 to 30 minutes).

Pour into clean sterilised containers.

Quince Butter

- 6 large quinces, peeled and cored
- 2 cups water

Place quince into food processor and mince. Place into a pot with the water and simmer until quince is soft and pulpy.

Weigh pulp. Place into pot with sugar measurement.

Bring slowly to the boil and stir until sugar has dissolved. Simmer stirring frequently until thick, with no excess liquid.

Pour into clean sterilised containers.

Quince Paste

Make as for Quince butter but continue cooking until the paste thickens and begins to come away from the bottom of the pan. Stir continually; be aware boiling paste will spit.

Take off heat and continue stirring until spitting stops. Pour paste into shallow baking dish and leave to cool.

Leave covered with cloth and place in a cylinder cupboard for a few days until dried. Slice into portions and glad wrap. Store in air tight container.

Lemon Honey

Lemon honey is also known as lemon curd, and is the filling used for lemon meringue pie.

Lemon honey folded into whipped cream or on top of ice-cream makes an instant dessert.

• 240 g butter • 1 cup lemon juice • 1 cup lime juice • 4 cups sugar

Place all the ingredients into the top of a double boiler (a saucepan with a heat-proof bowl placed over simmering water)

Stir until the sugar dissolves, then add • 12 beaten eggs.

Whisk altogether and continue cooking stirring or whisking periodically until the mixture thickens (about 30 minutes).

Pour into clean sterilised jars. Make sure the jars are not too hot as the egg may re-cook and curdle.

This product keeps in sealed jars for up to 6 months; once opened, refrigerate.

Lime juice can be replaced with lemon juice.

Orange Curd

Make as for lemon honey, replacing the lemon and lime juice with orange juice.

Passion Fruit Curd

Make as for lemon honey replacing the lime juice with the pulp of up to 12 sieved passion fruit.

Lemon Meringue Pie

- Pastry

- 250g flour • 60g caster sugar • Pinch salt • 180g butter • 2 egg yolks • Few drops water

In a food processor, combine the flour, sugar and salt, add butter, and process until it resembles breadcrumbs. Add egg yolks and water. Knead and cover. Refrigerate 1 hour. Roll out pastry, place in a pie dish, prick the base with a fork all over to prevent shrinkage, and bake for about 15 minutes or until lightly golden at 200C. Allow to cool.

Pour the lemon honey onto the base and spread evenly.

Meringue

- 3 egg whites • 100 g caster sugar

Beat 3 egg whites until stiffened, adding the sugar slowly until combined and forming stiff peaks.

Evenly spoon or pipe onto the lemon honey.

Bake in a hot oven 230C for a few minutes until the meringue is browned.

Specialties and Pickled

Christmas Mince

Christmas mince is used for making Christmas mince pies and fillings for slices.

- 1 kg cooking apples • 250 g currants
- 1 kg brown sugar
- Juice and grated rind of 1 grapefruit, lemon, and orange
- 2 tablespoons chopped crystallised ginger • 500 g sultanas
- ½ teaspoon ground cinnamon • ½ teaspoon ground nutmeg
- 100 g mixed peel, finely chopped • 1¼ litres water

Peel, core and slice apples, and place into a large pan with juice and rind, ginger, sultanas, currants, cinnamon, nutmeg, mixed peel and water. Bring to a boil and simmer until the apples are tender. Add the brown sugar and bring back to the boil for 15 minutes.

Add • 125 ml Brandy, • 100 ml Grand Marnier, • 1 cup whole almonds chopped.

Pour into clean sterilised jars. Wait for 2 months before using.

Elderflower Champagne

This is a very enjoyable drink.

This drink can be very fizzy, so do not over-fill bottles.

- 4 litres water • 2 ½ cups sugar • 8 heads of fresh elderflowers
- 2 lemons, sliced • 2 tablespoons white vinegar

Bring the water and sugar to the boil. Cool liquid and add the elderflower heads, sliced lemons and vinegar, and stir mixture.

Leave to sit for 24 hours covered, then strain and bottle, and leave for 1 to 2 weeks. For bottles, re-use lemonade or Coke plastic bottles.

Rhubarb Champagne

This drink can be very fizzy, so do not over-fill bottles.

- 850 g sugar • 850 g chopped rhubarb • 1 whole lemon, sliced
- 2 tablespoons white vinegar • 4 litres water

Place sugar and water to the boil. Cool add rhubarb, lemon and vinegar, and stir. Leave to stand for 2 days covered, stirring occasionally.

Strain and bottle, and leave for 2 weeks. For bottles, re-use lemonade or Coke plastic bottles.

Vegemite

- 250 g brewer's flaked yeast (not bread yeast or yeast granules)
- 2 tablespoons wheat germ • 350 ml soy sauce

Mix all ingredients and refrigerate.

Figs with Orange

Serve as a dessert with homemade mascarpone or yoghurt, enjoy over breakfast cereals, or on an antipasto cheese board - or have with hot and cold meats..

- 3 oranges, halved and thinly sliced
- 50 g crystallised ginger, chopped
- 300 mls white vinegar • 1½ litres water • 3 ½ kg sugar
- 1 teaspoon whole cloves

Bring all ingredients to the boil until sugar has dissolved.

Add:

- 6 kg fresh figs

Bring back to the simmer, and simmer gently for up to 2 hours or until figs are soft.

Pack into clean sterilised jars, add the cooking syrup until jars are full, wipe clean and seal.

Pickled Tamarillos

Pickled tamarillos go well with venison, cold meats, salads or on any cheese board.

- 3 litres white vinegar • 4.4 kg sugar
- 70 g ground cloves • 35 g ground cinnamon • 1 lemon peel skin

Place all ingredients into a pot, bring to the boil, and simmer for 15 minutes.

Divide mixture into 2 pots.

Peel tamarillos (helpful hint on page 14)

Place tamarillos into one of the pots; bring to a simmer, until the fruit is soft but not falling apart.

Carefully place the tamarillos into clean sterilised jars, and top up with the liquid mixture from the second simmering pot.

Seal jars.

Do not throw away liquid mixture: it makes excellent spiced vinegar to use in cooking or vinaigrettes and marinades.

Spiced Feijoas

- 2.5 litres white vinegar • 2.25 kg sugar • 40 g whole cloves
- 1 large fresh ginger, sliced thinly • 5 cinnamon sticks

Place all ingredients into a pot and bring to the boil. Simmer for 15 minutes. Divide mixture into 2 pots.

Peel feijoas

Place feijoas into one of the pots and bring to a simmer, until the fruit is soft but not falling apart.

Carefully place the feijoas into clean sterilised jars, and top up each jar with the liquid mixture from the second simmering pot.

Seal jars.

Do not throw away liquid mixture: it makes excellent spiced vinegar to use in cooking or vinaigrettes and marinades.

Pickled Cherries

Pickled cherries accompany antipasto dishes, salads, cold or hot meats.

- 2.5 litres white vinegar • 2.25 kg sugar • 40 g whole cloves
- 1 large fresh ginger, sliced thinly • 5 cinnamon sticks

Place all ingredients into a pot and bring to the boil; simmer for 15 minutes. Leave to go cool. Strain the liquid.

Place clean cherries into clean sterilised jars; pour in strained vinegar, seal and leave to marinate for 6 weeks.

Do not throw away liquid mixture: it makes excellent spiced vinegar to use in cooking or vinaigrettes and marinades.

Pickled Dill Cucumbers

- 1 kg small cucumbers

Clean cucumbers and soak for up to two days in brine.

- Brine • ¾ cup salt • 2.5 litres boiling water

Dissolve salt in boiling water. Cool before using.

Place cucumbers in brine. It is important to immerse and completely cover cucumbers - place a plate on them and use a weight to hold them down.

Rinse in clean cold water and drain well before packing into jars. Either leave the cucumbers whole, or sliced or cut in quarter's length ways.

Pack cucumbers into jars and place a • garlic clove, • dill head and leaves, and • 6 black peppercorns into each jar. Top up with the vinegar solution.

Vinegar

- 7 tablespoons rock salt • 6 black peppercorns
- 225 ml white vinegar • 750 ml water

Place vinegar, salt, peppercorns and water into a pot, bring to the boil. Leave to go cold.

Vinegar used cold with cucumbers will keep them crisp.

Seal jars. Date and label. Store for 6 weeks before using.

Pickled Onions

- 1 kg small onions

Peel and place onions in a bowl, and soak in brine over night

- Brine • ¾ cup salt • 2.5 litres boiling water

Dissolve salt in boiling water and pour over onions while hot.

Place onions in brine. It is important to immerse and completely cover onions- place a plate on them and use a weight to hold them down.

Drain well before packing into jars.

Vinegar

- 7 tablespoons rock salt • 1 tablespoon black peppercorns
- 225 ml white vinegar • 750 ml water • 25 g fresh ginger, chopped
- ¼ teaspoon ground mace (*page 30) • 1 tablespoon whole cloves

Place vinegar ingredients into a pot, bring to the boil. Leave to go cold.

Pour the vinegar solution over onions, overflow jars and seal.

Leave for 2 weeks before serving.

Oven-dried Tomatoes

Halve tomatoes and scoop out the seeds; place on oven tray and arrange skin side down, on tray. Sprinkle inside of tomatoes with salt.

Place in oven and dry at 60C with oven door open for up to 12 hours, or until tomatoes are dry and no liquid is showing when cut in half.

Place dried tomatoes into clean sterilised jars. To each jar add:

- 1 garlic clove   • 6 black peppercorns • 1 chilli (optional)

Herbs of choice either - tarragon, thyme, rosemary or oregano

Top up each jar with either olive oil or rice bran oil.

Press down to release air bubbles; wipe any trace of oil from rim and seal. Ready to use in 4 weeks.

Liqueurs and Brandied Fruit

Plum Liqueur

- 1 kg ripe plums complete with stones • 250g sugar

- 1 vanilla pod or 2 teaspoons vanilla essence • 1 litre rum or vodka

Squash plums. Place all ingredients into large bucket with a lid, and leave to macerate for 6 weeks.

Strain into clean sterilised bottles.

The solids can be bottled and used to fill desserts or enjoy over ice-cream.

Try adding a small amount to casseroles.

Coffee Liqueur

Mix • 250g ground coffee with • 1 litre of rum or vodka, leave to infuse for 2 weeks.

Syrup • 840g water • 560g sugar

Place syrup ingredients into a pot and bring to the boil. Leave to cool.

Add this to the coffee alcohol mixture. Leave to stand for 2 weeks.

Strain through a muslin bag and bottle.

Brandied Grapes

Place grapes in a bucket with a lid. Cover with brandy or vodka, leave to macerate for 3 weeks.

Strain grapes and place into clean sterilised jars. Retain the macerated alcohol.

Syrup • 500g sugar • 500mls water

Bring to the simmer until sugar has dissolved. Leave to cool.

Add the syrup to the alcohol mixture. Pour the syrup-alcohol mixture over the grapes, seal, and leave for 2 weeks.

This recipe can be used for red currants, raspberries, strawberries, blackberries and black currants.

For cherries, use the same recipe and add cinnamon quill and vanilla pod to the bucket.

Rum Fruit Pots

• Boysenberries, Raspberries, Blackberries • 1 litre rum • 300g sugar

Place into clean sterilised jars a mixture of the berries.

Slowly heat rum until sugar has dissolved, leave to cool.

Pour rum mixture over fruits. Seal jars and use after 1 month or more.

Delicious over ice-cream, folded into whipped cream, or eaten on its own. Serve with waffles, or place in a trifle.

Vinaigrettes and Pesto

Sun-Dried Tomato Pesto

Sun-dried tomato pesto goes well with crackers and cheese, or tossed into cooked pasta.

- 250 g sun-dried tomatoes • 20 g grated parmesan
- 600ml olive oil • 125 g walnuts • 15 g garlic
- 80 g fresh basil • 2 teaspoons sugar • ½ teaspoon salt

Put all ingredients into a blender and blend.

Place into containers or clean sterilised jars, and refrigerate.

Basil Pesto

Basil pesto goes well with crackers and cheese, on eggs and fish, with fresh or grilled tomatoes, or tossed into cooked pasta.

- 150 g (1 cup packed firmly) fresh basil - use the soft stalks too
- 350 ml olive oil
- 4 tablespoons grated parmesan
- 170 g walnuts • 3 cloves garlic
- 1 teaspoon salt

Put all ingredients into a blender and blend.

Place in container and refrigerate, or freeze into small serving-portion sizes.

Olive Pesto

Olive pesto goes well with crackers and cheese, on eggs, fish and grilled meats, fresh or grilled tomatoes, or tossed into cooked pasta.

- 1 cup whole olives, pitted • 1 cup fresh basil • 1 cup walnuts
- 1 tablespoon lemon juice • ½ teaspoon mustard powder
- 3 garlic cloves • 1 cup olive oil

Put all ingredients into a blender and blend.

Place in container and refrigerate.

Tapenade

This paste is spread on bread, toast and crackers, or used as a dip with raw vegetables. Try it with boiled eggs on toast.

- 50 g anchovies • 50 g tin tuna, drained • 50 g capers
- 125 g pitted whole olives • 1 clove garlic • Juice of one lemon
- 1 teaspoon fresh thyme or ½ teaspoon dried thyme
- 3 tablespoons olive oil - or enough to form a paste

Place all Ingredients into a blender and process into a paste.

Place into clean sterilised jars and refrigerate.

This will keep well for several weeks.

To add an aromatic, include a drop of brandy.

Anchovy Vinaigrette

Excellent vinaigrette on hot or cold vegetables or salads

- 200 g anchovy mustard mix (see page 35)
- 800 ml olive oil or rice bran oil or oil of choice • 400 ml white vinegar
- 60 g anchovies • 2 teaspoons salt • 1 teaspoon ground black pepper

Put all ingredients into a blender and blend.

When completely blended, bottle into clean cooled sterilised jars.

Tamari and Ginger Dressing

Tamari ginger dressing makes an excellent marinade for chicken, lamb and beef.

Enjoy on cold salads and hot vegetables, or blend through a stir fry of vegetables.

- 200 g fresh ginger • 80 g garlic, peeled • 400ml white vinegar

Place ingredients into a blender and blend until you have a puree.

Add to this

- 100ml Tamari (Soy) • 500ml liquid honey • 350ml boiled cooled water
- 1.5 litres olive oil or rice bran oil or oil of choice

Blend altogether, bottle into clean cooled sterilised jars.

Sun-Dried Tomato Vinaigrette

Excellent vinaigrette on hot or cold vegetables or salads, or drizzled over eggs.

- 100 g sun-dried tomatoes
- 35 g garlic, peeled
- 1 cup fresh basil or ¼ cup dried basil
- 1.7 litres olive oil or rice bran oil or oil of choice
- 300 ml balsamic vinegar
- 2 teaspoons salt • 2 teaspoons sugar
- 1 teaspoon ground black peppercorns

Put all ingredients except the oil into a blender and blend until a pulp, then add oil slowly to mix.

Blend all together, and bottle into clean cooled sterilised jars.

Herbal oils and vinegars

Herbal Oils

Herbal oils are especially delicious in cooking and an excellent way to preserve fresh herbs like basil when out of season.

It is important to use dry herbs, as the water from fresh herbs can cause mould.

Take 1/2 cup of olive, vegetable or rice bran oil. Hard-pack 1 cup of fresh herbs, and process in the blender with the oil.

Alternatively, finely chop the herbs, and add to the oil Bottle.

For longer storage it is important to store fresh herb oil, refrigerate or freeze. In the case of basil oil, freezing is recommended.

Gourmet herbal oils:

Place into a plain or fancy bottle 6 peppercorns, 6 dried chillies, garlic, olives and sundried tomatoes (optional).

Fill with olive oil, vegetable oil or rice bran oil. Leave in a cool dark place for between a week and a month, to infuse.

Flavoured oils are excellent as a dip with breads, or for grilling, basting and frying.

Herbs to use for gourmet oils

For savoury use: basil, garlic, fennel, marjoram, mint, rosemary, tarragon, thyme, savory.

For sweet use: lavender, lemon verbena, rose petals.

Herbal Vinegars:

Herbal vinegars are flavoured vinegars for use in salad dressings, marinades, gravies and sauces or for adding to poached-egg water.

To make tarragon vinegar, place in a plain or fancy bottle:

Peppercorns, dried or fresh chilli, mustard seeds and a large sprig of fresh tarragon.

Use your imagination to create many other interesting flavours.

Herbs for vinegars

Basil, Chervil, Dill, Fennel, Garlic, Lemon Balm, Marjoram, Mint, Rosemary, Savoury, Thyme.

Flowers for vinegars

Carnations, Clover, Elderflowers, Lavender, Nasturtiums, Rose petals, Rosemary flowers, Thyme flowers and sweet violets.

Preserving Fruit and Vegetables

Process of preservation is to slow down and stop natural bacteria deterioration - mainly Clostridium botulinum - occurring.

Bacteria grow at temperatures between 4C and 63C. To prevent bacteria in your preserves, temperatures must be heated and maintained at 75C to 130C for long enough for the heat to reach the centre of the fruits in the jars.

As a guide, time ratios are stated in each method.

Sterilise Jars

Visually check jars for nicks, cracks and for uneven smooth rims that will prevent the lids from sealing.

Wash jars, lids and rims. In a home kitchen place jars in the oven at 100C for 15 minutes or more to sterilise.

Out at sea, sterilise jars in a large pot filled with water to cover jars, and boil for 15 minutes.

Place lids and rims in a pot of boiling water, turn off heat and leave in pot.

Always maintain clean and sterilised equipment to guard against cross contamination and the natural microorganisms present in the air we breathe such as, moulds, yeast and bacteria.

Syrup

Light syrup: 1 cup of sugar to 3 cups of water

Medium syrup: 1 ½ cups sugar to 3 cups of water

Heavy syrup: 2 cups sugar to 2 cups of water

Fruits have natural sugar and can be preserved without adding further sugar; just add boiling water. Sweetener or sugar can be added before serving.

Brine method for vegetables

To each medium preserving jar add ½ to 1 teaspoon of salt and top up with boiling water. Proceed as for water bath and low-acid food methods.

Oven Method

This method involves placing fruit in a beautifully orderly fashion into sterilised jars with boiling syrup. The lids are loosely placed on the jars, and the jars are placed on the second shelf from the bottom of the oven with the temperature at 140C. The jars must not touch each other or the oven walls.

Tighten down lids as you remove jars from the oven.

Times depend on fruit sizes:

Small fruits about 20 minutes;

Medium to large fruits and tomatoes about 30 to 45 minutes.

This process is used for fruits and tomatoes only.

Water-Bath Method

The Water-bath method can be used instead of the oven method for preserving fruits.

Water-bath is the way to preserve vegetables, meat and fish that are low acid foods.

Note: To obtain optimum heat and pressure, a pressure cooker should be used, for best results. Go to Low Acid Method page 93.

This method requires a large pot with a trivet or cloth or rack to keep the jars off the bottom. The pot must be deep enough to cover the top of the jars and the pot must have a fitting lid.

Pour water into the pot that is at about the same temperature as the syrup in the jars.

Place fruit in a beautifully orderly fashion into sterilised jars with boiling syrup, or boiling water.

Screw lids on jars firmly and then release half a turn. Place jars into pot. Jars must not be touching each other or sides of pot and process.

Screw lids on jars firmly and then release half a turn.

Cooking time starts when the water has come to the boil; it must then be kept at a boil. Tighten down lids as you remove jars from the water-bath.

Process time below

Times for water-bath method:

Small fruits up to 30 minutes

Medium to large fruits up to 50 minutes

Vegetables up to 3 hours

Fish up to 4 hours.

Open Pot Method

For this method, add fruit to hot syrup (page 91) and cook until tender. When tender, gently lift out fruit and place into clean sterilised jars. Top up each jar with an extra pot of the syrup simmering on stove to overflow the jars slightly. Clean jars and seal.

I found this method the simplest. It may not give you a visual symphony of carefully-placed fruits, but it is quick and avoids the odd jars cracking, which can occur in the oven and water-bath method.

NB: This method is for fruits and tomatoes only.

Low-Acid Foods

This method was given to me by a sailor friend Jan, who used it successfully for preserving meats on her extended sailing trips. Jan shared her knowledge with me on canning - or "jarring" - for others on their long voyages.

Jan would make up batches of casseroled or stewed meats, I.e. Sweet and sour chicken, ham off the bone in a brine, mince (plain - flavours were added later), beef stew plain – flavour added later to make beef stroganoff, UHT cream and tinned mushroom.

Jan only ever had one jar that was suspect. As the lid did not release suction when opened, Jan did a finger taste test and found the taste was metallic. Be aware: if in doubt PLEASE THROW OUT. Spoilage organisms Clostridium botulinum can be present in any foods but they thrive in a moist, low-acid environment without the presence of air. To prevent this, filled jars are processed at a temperature of 130C for a period of time. Jan found to maintain consistent heat, the pressure cooker method was the best canning or jarring technique; the water-bath method only reaches the temperature of boiling water, which is not enough for low-acid foods. Jan used a 9 litre pressure cooker which held three one litre preserving jars. This method is also used for vegetables and seafood.

Low acid foods which are mixed with high acid foods - such as tomatoes with meat or vegetables - are still considered low acid foods.

Home canning is simple, providing correct steps are followed to ensure the application of the heat process to food in a closed jar for a period of time to ensure the destruction of microorganisms.

Preparation: the ten easy steps

1. Tools required: three or four clean dish towels and cloths: a large pot or an oven to sterilise jars: tongs and a food funnel or large spoon, scoop or ladle to transfer hot food into jars. Spatula or knife to remove air bubbles.

Appropriate preserving jars and lids. Jar tongs to place and lift out jars from pressure cooker.

Pressure cooker.

2. Visually check jars: for nicks, cracks and for uneven smooth rims that will prevent the lids from sealing.

Wash jars, lids and rims. In a home kitchen place jars in an oven at 100C for 15 minutes or more to sterilise.

(Out at sea, sterilise jars in a large pot filled with water to cover jars and boil for 15 minutes.)

Place lids and rims in a pot of boiling water, turn off heat and leave in pot. Do not boil lids.

Always maintain clean and sterilised equipment to prevent cross contamination and the entry of natural microorganisms present in the air we breathe such as moulds, yeast, and bacteria.

Sterilise dish cloths in 1 litre warm water with 50 mls bleach; these are used to wipe jar rims.

3. Prepare food for canning: make up food for canning, mince, vegetables or stews.

4. Filling jars: while still hot, ladle into hot sterilised jars taking care to get as little food as possible outside of the jar or on the rim. Fill jar from 15 mm to 25 mm from rim to allow for expansion of the contents, and pack it firmly, running a knife or spatula around inside the jar to push contents down and to release air bubbles.

5. Sealing jars: Clean rims with sterilised cloth, place a sterilised seal onto the jar, and screw down the band until it is just a little tighter than finger-tight, to allow the contents in the jar to expand and release air and some contents during processing. The band should not be screwed down too tightly.

6. Processing the jars: Place jars onto a trivet to keep them off the bottom of the pressure cooker. If you do not have a trivet fold a towel and place the jars on the towel, spacing them evenly on the trivet or towel in the pressure cooker. Jars must not touch the sides of the pressure cooker or each other.

Fill pressure cooker up to ¾ of the level of the jars with hot water, lock down pressure cooker lid.

Time starts when the pounds of pressure is reached in your pressure cooker manual. Adjust heat to achieve and maintain recommended pressure shown in your pressure cooker manual.

7. Recommended times: Chicken, turkey and lamb - Remove all fat from lamb as the fat will make the meat taste rancid.

Cook poultry or lamb until nearly cooked, season with salt, pepper or spices, water or meat juice and process for 1 hour at 10 to 15 pounds of pressure.

Stews and soups - Cook soups and stews until nearly cooked: process 45 to 60 minutes at 10 to 15 pounds of pressure.

Fish -Place ¼ to ½ teaspoon of salt or vinegar in the bottom of the jar, fillet fish and remove skin. Place raw fish in jar with 1 tablespoon of olive oil, and top up with water. Process for 90 minutes at 10 to 15 pounds of pressure.

Tuna - Pre-cook tuna to remove strong-tasting oils. Place cooked tuna into jars with salt or vinegar, spices and olive oil, and top with water. Process for 90 minutes at 10 to 15 pounds of pressure.

8. Cooling jars: when jars have completed processing, take off heat and leave to cool down.

Canning Problems occur when jars cool down too quickly. Leave them in the pressure cooker to cool overnight; if you need to process additional foods, remove jars when the pressure cooker has cooled enough to let you remove them with your bare hands. Wrap each jar to keep it warm to keep it from cooling down too quickly.

9. Testing seal: When the jars have cooled completely, test the seal visually, by looking across the lid to see if the lid has concaved (inverted inwards); by feel - place your thumb on the lid which shouldn't give or spring back; and by tapping the lid with a spoon - the lid should sound high-pitched, not dull and flat.

Do Not re-screw down the lids.

If any jars are suspect, open and consume now, or place in a clean sterilised jar to reprocess.

10. Label and stow: label and date jars. (To protect jars out at sea, Jan places each jar in a sock and stows in a plastic container lined with plastic or newspaper.)

Final test: Visually check jar seal and listen for the sound when the jar is opened. Make sure when you open a jar that you hear the hissing sound made when the vacuum is broken; this is the final test to ensure the contents are good and ready to eat.

Fresh Chutneys and Sauces

Feijoa Salsa

Serve with steak, duck or chicken

- 12 feijoas, roughly chopped • Zest of 4 lemons or limes
- 2 spring onions, chopped finely
- 2 teaspoons sweet chilli sauce or finely chopped fresh chilli
- 4 medium tomatoes, peeled de-seeded and diced
- 1 tablespoon balsamic vinegar • 2 tablespoons chopped parsley
- ¼ cup oil • Salt pepper

Mix altogether and chill for at least 1 hour and preferably 3 hours.

Cranberry Chutney

This chutney goes well with turkey, pork and wild game and can be prepared a week ahead.

Dried cranberries can be used: add an extra one cup of cranberry juice to the recipe;

- 1 ½ cups fresh cranberries • 100 g dried apricots, lightly chopped
- ¾ cup brown sugar • ¼ cup currants
- 2 tablespoons fresh ginger, grated • ¾ teaspoon ground cinnamon
- ¼ teaspoon cayenne pepper • ¼ cup cranberry juice

Place all ingredients in a saucepan. Cook over medium heat until sugar has dissolved. Bring to a boil and boil for 3 minutes.

Pour into a clean sterilised jar and refrigerate.

Tomato Capsicum Chutney

This chutney goes well as a dip, placed in an open sandwich or with savoury muffins.

Have it with fresh bread and cheese.

Use as an alternative to gravy with roast meat, chicken, pork or fish.

- 4 tomatoes, roasted and skinned
- 2 red capsicums roasted, de-seeded and skinned
- 2 red chillies roasted, de-seeded and skinned
- 4 cloves garlic, peeled and crushed fresh or slightly roasted
- 1 tablespoon red wine vinegar • ½ cup toasted almond
- Salt and pepper to taste • 75 mls extra virgin olive oil
- 1 cup fresh herbs either coriander, basil, parsley or a mixture.

Place into a blender and blend. For a slightly thicker sauce or to extend the sauce, add 1 slice of bread and blend, adjusting oil quantity as required.

Carrot Chutney

This chutney goes well with lamb or chicken, with pita breads or as a dip with nachos.

- 1 kg cooked carrots • 3 cloves garlic, peeled and crushed
- ¼ teaspoon cayenne powder • 1 teaspoon turmeric
- 1 teaspoon ground cumin • ½ teaspoon ground ginger
- 1 teaspoon paprika • 1 tablespoon honey
- 2 tablespoons lemon juice • 50mls extra virgin olive oil

Place all ingredients into a blender and blend, or mash with a potato masher until well mashed.

Lemon Dressing

- 2 tablespoons lemon juice • 6 tablespoons olive oil or rice bran oil
- ½ teaspoon salt • 1 teaspoon whole grain mustard • Black pepper

Whisk all ingredients together.

Use in salads or drizzle over cooked fish.

Mint Sauce

- ¾ cup fresh mint leaves chopped • ½ cup water
- 1 cup malt vinegar • ⅓ cup sugar

Combine sugar, vinegar and water in a saucepan. Bring to the boil and simmer for 4 minutes.

Take off heat and add chopped mint leaves.

Coriander Mint Sauce

- 1 cup natural yoghurt • 2 tablespoons chopped coriander
- 2 tablespoons chopped mint leaves • 1 tablespoon liquid honey
- Salt & pepper • 1 clove garlic, crushed
- ½ teaspoon sweet chilli sauce or a few drops Tabasco sauce.

Mix all ingredients and chill for a few hours.

Mango Dressing

This sauce goes well with fish and fish cakes.

- Juice of 1 large lemon • 250 ml rice bran oil or vegetable oil
- 2 teaspoons fish sauce • Zest and juice of 3 limes
- 1 ripe mango, peeled and stoned • 1 garlic clove
- 3 cm piece fresh ginger, peeled • 2 medium fresh chillies
- 1 cup fresh coriander • ½ cup mint leaves

Place all ingredients in a blender and blend, then refrigerate - will keep for up to two days.

Thai Fish Cakes

- 500 g fish fillets • 2 small chillies
- 2 cloves garlic • Lemon grass (optional)
- 2 tablespoons coriander leaves
- 1 tablespoon fish sauce
- 1 egg • ¼ cup coconut milk

Process in blender, make into patties and chill.

Fry for about 2 minutes each side; don't over-cook.

Avocado Dip

- 2 ripe avocados • 2 tablespoons lemon juice
- 1 garlic clove, minced • 2 tablespoons onion, finely chopped
- ½ cup of chopped coriander leaves • 2 tablespoons chopped red chilli
- 1 tomato with seeds removed, chopped finely.
- Salt and pepper to taste.

Scoop out the flesh from the avocados and mash. Add all remaining ingredients, and mix well.

Serve with rice crackers, corn chips or vegetable sticks.

Mayonnaise and Sauce

Mayonnaise made in blender

- 1 whole egg
- 2 teaspoons white wine vinegar
- ½ teaspoon salt

- 300ml of either olive, rice bran, or sunflower oil, or use a mixture according to your preference.

Place egg, vinegar, and salt into liquidiser or blender, blend and slowly add the oil until mixture has emulsified. Do not rush the first 150 mls of oil as the mixture can separate.

Mustard Mayonnaise

Make mayonnaise in blender. Add to this 1 teaspoon mustard powder and blend.

Lemon Mayonnaise

Make the mayonnaise in blender, replacing the vinegar with 1 tablespoon lemon juice and finely grated lemon zest.

Herb Mayonnaise

Make mayonnaise in blender. Add ¼ to ½ cup fresh finely chopped herbs of choice: basil, tarragon, chervil, parsley, calendula petals, rose petals, mint, chives or a mixture.

Cocktail Sauce 1

This sauce is enjoyed with a seafood or prawn cocktail.

- ½ cup mayonnaise • 3 tablespoons tomato sauce
- ½ teaspoon Tabasco sauce or Worcestershire sauce
- Salt/pepper

Mix the above ingredients in a bowl.

Cocktail Sauce 2

This sauce is a lighter version of the cocktail sauce 1.

- ½ cup mayonnaise • 3 tablespoons tomato sauce
- ½ teaspoons Tabasco sauce or Worcestershire sauce
- Salt/pepper • ½ cup whipped cream

Mix the above ingredients in a bowl.

Cocktail Sauce 3

Make as for cocktail sauce 2, replacing the whipped cream with plain yoghurt.

Tartare Sauce

This sauce is enjoyed with all types of fish.

- ½ cup mayonnaise • 1 teaspoon chopped olives
- 1 teaspoon chopped gherkins • 1 teaspoon chopped capers
- 2 teaspoons chopped chives • Salt/pepper
- 2 teaspoons chopped fresh tarragon, chervil or parsley

Mix the above ingredients in a bowl.

Béarnaise Sauce

This sauce is a reduction of vinegar or wine and herbs. This is then added to the made-up hollandaise sauce.

In a pot, place:

- 1 dessertspoon chopped herbs: either tarragon, chervil, or a mixture
- 1 small onion, chopped
- ½ teaspoon of ground black pepper
- 50 mls of vinegar or wine.

Boil rapidly until reduced to 1 tablespoon. Either strain or leave as is. Add slowly to the hollandaise sauce and mix.

This sauce takes away the richness of the butter in the hollandaise sauce and adds more piquancy.

Hollandaise made in blender

This is a quick way to make hollandaise. Hollandaise sauce is served with cooked fish, poached eggs, boiled or steamed vegetables.

- 2 tablespoons water • 2 egg yolks
- 225g clarified butter warmed (page 109) • Juice ½ lemon
- Large pinch cayenne pepper • ¾ teaspoon salt

Place water, egg yolks, lemon juice, cayenne pepper and salt in blender and blend, slowly pouring in the warmed clarified butter.

This sauce will hold for up to 2 hours covered and in a warm place.

If the sauce splits or curdles, it can be re-emulsified by adding warm water drop by drop.

If the sauce is cold use hot water and use cold water if the sauce is hot.

Dairy Products

Mascarpone, Crème Fraiche and Ricotta are simple and cheap to make. It will give you great pleasure to share with others that you have created these products from scratch.

Sterilize containers with 50mls of bleach added to 1 litre of water.

Mascarpone

- 1 litre cream • ½ teaspoon tartaric acid

To make mascarpone: scald cream, cool, and add tartaric acid, leave overnight to set in fridge.

Line a sieve with damp muslin or a clean Chux cloth.

Pour mixture into sieve, place in fridge and drain overnight or until the whey has stopped dripping. Place in clean container. Mascarpone will keep for 2 weeks. Makes 500ml.

Crème Fraiche

• 500 ml cream • 250 ml buttermilk or sour milk

Gently heat the cream and buttermilk until just below body temp (25C). Pour the cream into a container and partly cover. Keep at room temperature for 6-8 hours or until it has thickened and tastes slightly acid.

The cream will thicken faster on a hot day.

Stir and store in the refrigerator for up to 2 weeks. Makes 750ml.

Ricotta

• 2 litres milk • ¼ cup vinegar • Salt

Place milk in a 4 litre double boiler, and add salt to taste.

Heat slowly to 85C. When it has reached this temperature, stir the heated milk very, very slowly (snail's pace) while adding vinegar. Stop stirring as soon as the curd has formed.

Gently scoop out the curd into a lined colander and allow it to cool, then place in a clean container. Ricotta can be used immediately; otherwise store it in the refrigerator.

Cottage Cheese

• 1 litre milk • 2 teaspoons rennet (page 108)

Heat milk to lukewarm and remove from heat. Add rennet, stir slowly for thirty seconds, and allow to set.

Break up the curd and put it into a sieve lined with muslin or a Chux cloth. Stand overnight to separate the curds and whey. Place in a clean container; it can be used immediately or stored in the refrigerator.

Sour Cream (1)

• 1 cup cream • 1 tablespoon buttermilk

Recipe can be increased: just keep doubling ingredients.

In a double boiler bring cream up to bubble-froth stage. Cool to room temperature, in a cold-water bath in the sink.

Add buttermilk, cover and let stand for 24 to 48 hours. Stir and place into clean container and refrigerate. This will keep for up to 3 to 4 weeks.

Sour Cream (2)

- 1 cup cream • ¼ cup of original sour cream culture or buttermilk

Put all ingredients into a screw-top jar and stand at room temperature for 24 hours until thick.

Refrigerate.

Note: Buttermilk is a by-product of butter-making (page 109). It freezes and can be used for cooking - but not drinking! - when frozen.

Yoghurt

- 1 litre milk; any kind
- 3 Tablespoons non-fat dried milk powder (optional)

Starter: 2 tablespoons existing yogurt with live cultures,

i.e. natural yogurt or acidophilus yogurt.

Whisk milk powder into a little of the milk until completely dissolved; this will help thicken the yoghurt more easily and add more nutrition. Then add rest of milk, and stir.

Heat the milk until it starts to froth or the temperature reaches 85C. Do not boil or burn the milk. Microwaving is good: it takes 8 to 10 minutes on high, depending on the microwave wattage.

Cool the milk to room temperature or baby-milk temperature. Add the starter yoghurt to the cooled milk.

Keep the yoghurt warm in either a yoghurt maker or an Easy-Yo container. Or you could use an oven where the temperature is maintained at 38C (having the oven light on might be enough); or in a double boiler - or maybe put it in your car on a sunny day. Just use your common sense and a thermometer.

After 8 hours the yoghurt should have a thickish appearance, and the whey - a thin yellow liquid - will form on top. You can pour off the whey or stir into yoghurt.

Refrigerated, this yoghurt will keep for 1 to 2 weeks.

Use 2 tablespoons of this yoghurt to create the next yoghurt within 5 days to keep the bacteria growing.

Yoghurt Cream Cheese

- 1kg plain yoghurt

Put yoghurt in a sieve lined with muslin or a Chux cloth, place over a bowl, and leave in the fridge for about 1 to 2 days to drain. Once drained, place in clean containers.

The drained liquid is called whey and the solid part is called curds. Have the curds as plain cream cheese, or add herbs, spices, jams, fresh fruit and nuts to create a tasty cheese spread.

Whey is full of amazing enzymes: add it to your soup, pikelets, pancakes, and muffins.

Yoghurt Iceblocks

Place yoghurt into small plastic cup containers or iceblock containers. Pureed fruit or chopped fruit can be added to the yogurt to make fruit-filled yogurt blocks.

To centre the all-important popsicle stick, place tin foil over container and poke popsicle stick through the middle. Freeze.

Cream Cheese

- 2 litres milk • ¼ cup buttermilk

Heat milk over low heat until lukewarm, take off heat and add buttermilk. Cover and leave to stand at room temperature until mixture has formed into a soft curd - about 24 hours.

Line a sieve with damp muslin or a clean Chux cloth.

Pour mixture into sieve and drain until the whey has stopped dripping - about 10 minutes. Fold cloth around curd to cover, place the sieve in a bowl to drain further and place in refrigerator for 8 to 24 hours until thick cheese forms.

Place cream cheese into a clean covered container.

Rennet

Liquid vegetarian rennet can be made from stinging nettle or whole dandelion plant and flowers. Put a large bunch in a pot, cover and bring to boil. Leave to cool for 2 hours and use a tablespoon of the liquid.

Rennet also comes from the white sap of figs, lemon juice, white vinegar, citric acid. These can all be used in cheese-making, though they will not make a hard cheese. For that, you'll need commercial rennet.

Sour Cream Dip

- 250g (1 cup) sour cream • Salt and pepper to taste.

Chopped herbs of your choice: chives, coriander, tarragon, dill, spring onions: you may want to add calendula petals for character.

Cottage Cheese and Tuna Spread

- 1 cup cottage cheese • 1 tin tuna, drained
- 2 medium or 1 large stalk of celery, chopped
- 2 tablespoons mayonnaise

Mix all together and use as a filling for sandwiches.

Roll it in fresh sandwich bread as an alternative to asparagus rolls.

Use it as a dip, or as a potato alternative.

Ricotta Terrine

- 1 kg ricotta • 3 eggs, beaten

3 tablespoons chopped herbs (make a mixture from the following: chives, marjoram, oregano, tarragon, parsley, salad burnet).

Place ricotta in a bowl and beat until smooth, then add the beaten eggs and mix into ricotta. Add the chopped herbs and fold into the mixture.

Place into a terrine or a loaf tin, and stand this tin in a basin of water.

Bake for 30 – 40 minutes at 180c

Place on a platter drizzled with olive oil sprinkled either with paprika or chopped herbs and serve with a salad and ciabatta bread.

Butter

Butter is very easy to make. The ingredients for butter are cream and a little salt. Place cream on bench to reach room temperature, around 20c.

Place cream in food processor or in cake mixer – beat as for whipping cream, keep processing the cream it will turn to a slight yellow colour and then little lumps of butter appear and a thin liquid called buttermilk. The butter will separate from the buttermilk.

Drain the buttermilk off – use in scones or baking or to make crème fraiche, sour cream and cream cheese.

Place cold water in processor or mixer operate on low speed for a minute to wash the butter, drain of the water and repeat process until water is really clean- you will need to do this process a few times- make sure water is cold or you will melt the butter.

It is important to have the butter well washed and the water clean- if not the butter will turn rancid. Place butter in a lined colander - you need to press the butter to remove all the water out of the butter, use your hands and press the water out.

When the water has been removed add up to ½ teaspoon of salt to 250g of butter and mix.

Wrap in cling film or grease proof paper and refrigerate or freeze.

Clarified Butter

Clarified butter is ordinary butter melted gently to separate the water, salt and milk solids. The extract is butterfat. This is excellent to use in shallow frying, braising and sautéing.

Covered this keeps well in a refrigerator up to six months.

Melt some butter gently, do not stir. Remove any scum build-up on the surface. Carefully pour the clear butter into a container leaving behind the milky by product.

Conversion Chart

All measurements throughout this book are level and are based on New Zealand measures.

Approximate conversions

Ounces	1	2	3	4	5	6	7	8
Grams	25	50	75	125	150	175	200	225

Ounces	9	10	11	12	13	14	15	16
Grams	250	275	325	350	375	400	450	500

Volumes

1,000ml equals 1 litre equals approx 2 pints

1 metric cup	= 250ml
1 metric teaspoon	= 15ml
1 metric dessertspoon	= 10ml
1 metric teaspoon	= 5ml

Oven Temperature

Thermostatic oven temperatures, reduce temperature from 10 to 25 degrees for thermo wave ovens; generally refer to the book supplied with your oven.

Celsius

| 130 | 140 | 160 | 180 | 190 | 200 | 215 | 230 | 245 | 260 |

Fahrenheit

| 260 | 290 | 325 | 350 | 375 | 400 | 425 | 450 | 475 | 500 |

Index

Preparation of Chutney 8	Feijoa and Ginger Jam 54	**Herbal Oils and Vinegars** 88
Safe Food Practices 9	Melon and Ginger Jam 51	Gourmet herbal oils 89
Chutney and Relishes 11	Pear and Ginger Jam 52	Herbal Oils 89
Ajvar 15	Strawberry and Rhubarb Jam 54	Flowers for vinegars 89
Apricot Chutney page 11	Strawberry Jam 55	Herbal Vinegars 89
Aubergine and Capsicum Relish 21	Summer Berry Jam 52	
Banana and Date Chutney 20		**Preserving Fruit and Vegetables** 90
Beetroot and Orange Chutney 25	**Jellies** 59	Syrup 91
Brinjal Pickle 18	Jelly Preparation 59	Brine 91
Carrot and Mustard Seed Chutney 24	Herb Jellies, Mint, Thyme & Marjoram 60	Method-Oven-Water Bath 91-92
Cherry Chutney 11	Crab Apple Jelly 63	Open Pot Method 92
Chilli Jam 22	Feijoa Jelly 61	Low-Acid Foods 93-95
Feijoa Chutney 12	Grape Jelly 64	
Green Tomato Chutney 27	Hawthorn Jelly 62	**Fresh Fruit and Chutneys** 96
Hot Indian Relish 17	Lemon Verbena Jelly 61	Avocado Dip 99
Kiwifruit Chutney 26	Loquat Jelly 64	Carrot Chutney 98
Lime and Date Chutney 23	Quince Jelly 63	Coriander Mint Sauce 98
Maharajah's Relish 17	Rose Geranium Jelly 61	Cranberry Chutney 97
Onion Marmalade 21	Rose Petal Jelly 62	Feijoa Salsa 96
Pear Chutney 12		Fresh Chutneys and Sauces 96
Plum Chutney 13	**Syrups** 67	Lemon Dressing 98
Prune and Apple Chutney 13	Blackberry Syrup 69	Mango Dressing 99
Quince Chutney 24	Black Currant Syrup 68	Mint Sauce 98
Ratatouille Chutney 19	Grape Juice 68	Thai Fish Cakes 99
Rhubarb Chutney 20	Lemon Syrup 67	Tomato Capsicum Chutney 97
Tamarillo Chutney 14	Orange Syrup 68	
Tamarind Relish 16	Rose Hip Syrup 67	**Mayonnaise and Sauce** 101
Zucchini Chutney 19	Strawberry Sauce 69	Béarnaise Sauce 103
		Cocktail Sauce 1 102
Sauce 29	**Fruit Butters and Pastes** 71	Cocktail Sauce 2 102
Blackboy Peach or Plum Sauce 30	Apple and Blackberry Butter 72	Cocktail Sauce 3 102
Garlic Sauce 29	Plum Butter 72	Herb Mayonnaise 101
Red Tomato Sauce 31	Plum Paste 72	Hollandaise made in blender 103
Rhubarb Chilli Sauce 29	Quince Butter 73	Lemon Mayonnaise 101
Tomato Sauce 30	Quince Paste 73	Mayonnaise made in blender 101
		Mustard Mayonnaise 101
Mustards 33	**Curds** 74	Tartare Sauce 102
Anchovy Mustard 35	Lemon Honey 74	
Green Peppercorn Mustard 36	Orange Curd 75	**Dairy Products** 104
Guinness Mustard 35	Passion Fruit Curd 75	Butter 109
Herb and Spice Mustard 34		Cottage Cheese 105
Mustard Fruits 37	**Specialties and Pickled** 77	Clarified Butter 109
Pine nut and Almond Mustard 33	Christmas Mince 77	Cream Cheese 107
Red Wine Mustard 34	Elderflower Champagne 77	Crème Fraiche 105
	Figs with Orange 78	Mascarpone 104
Jam – Conserves- Marmalades- Jellies	Oven-dried Tomatoes 81	Rennet 108
Preparation of Jams 39	Pickled Tamarillos 79	Ricotta 105
Pectin 40	Pickled Cherries 80	Sour Cream (1) 105
Home-made pectin 41	Pickled Dill Cucumbers 80	Sour Cream (2) 106
Acid in jams 41	Pickled Onions 81	Yoghurt 106
Problems with fruit and jam 41	Rhubarb Champagne 78	Yoghurt Cream Cheese 107
	Spiced Feijoas 79	
Conserve 43	Vegemite 78	**Miscellaneous**
Blueberry & Grand Marnier Conserve 44		Coconut Bread 49
Boysenberry & Cointreau Conserve 43	**Liqueurs and Brandied Fruit** 82	Cottage Cheese & Tuna Spread 108
Cherry and Kirsch Conserve 43	Brandied Grapes 83	Home-made Sponge with conserve 45
	Coffee Liqueur 83	Jam Tarts 55
Marmalade 47	Plum Liqueur 82	Lemon Meringue Pie 75
Grapefruit and Ginger Marmalade 47	Rum Fruit Pots 83	Orange Marmalade Cake 49
Lime Marmalade 48		Ricotta Terrine 108
Orange and Almond Marmalade 47	**Vinaigrettes and Pesto** 85	Savoury Scones with Chutney 56
	Anchovy Vinaigrette 86	Scones with Home-made Jam 56
Jams	Basil Pesto 85	Soda Bread 26
Apple and Chocolate Jam 57	Olive Pesto 86	Sour Cream Dip 108
Apricot Jam 53	Sun-Dried Tomato Pesto 85	Steamed Sponge Pudding with Jelly 65
Berry Jam with Stevia 57	Sun-Dried Tomato Vinaigrette 87	Suzanne's Lime chilli cheesecake 23
Blackcurrant Jam 54	Tamari and Ginger Dressing 87	Thai Fish Cakes 99
Black Doris Jam 53	Tapenade 86	Yoghurt Iceblocks 107

Author's note

Suzanne

I was just an ordinary person, living a normal existence ... or so I thought ... until I had a near-death experience in a head-on car collision, after the opposing driver fell asleep.

This accident catapulted me onto an incredible journey, which saw me taking on the legal system and processing my own documents for the courts; and even taking a lawyer – successfully - to the Law Society. I even found myself re-evaluating my own marriage!

The legal system that is inflicted on many individuals can become an incredible nightmare, a system that can be unfair and flawed by greedy manipulative legal teams.

Through all this, I found my way onto the solid road of the inner spirit; one's very own path to understanding and opening up to one's inner-consciousness.

I delight in teaching others "to harvest the self": that a correct relationship with oneself is of primary importance. From this can flow correct relationships with others and trust in the divine source.

But aside from all of this, my passion is my love of natural products - and teaching others about what is around us all. This brought about my first book "Back to Basics" and now this follow-up, "Back to Basics Harvest"

I am a motivational speaker, focussing on how to on how to overcome obstacles and create a vision and trust in the inner consciousness of the self.